MASTER SYMBOL
OF THE
SOLAR CROSS

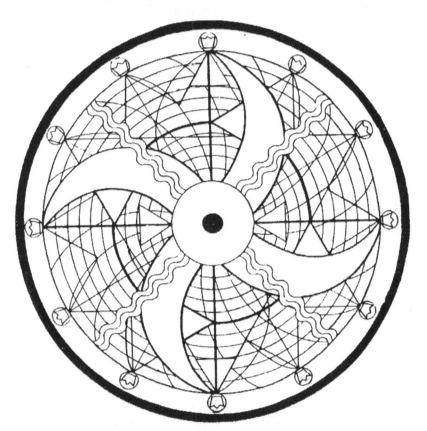

Compiled by Tarvis
With Channeling by Tuella
Representative of the Ashtar Command

Inner Light/Global Communications

MASTER SYMBOL OF THE SOLAR CROSS

TARVIS, COMPILER
TUELLA, CHANNELER
ASHTAR COMMAND

EAN: 978-1-60611-016-4
ISBN: 1-60611-016-0

Nonfiction

Timothy Green Beckley: Editorial Director
Carol Rodriguez: Publishers Assistant
Sean Casteel: Associate Editor

Printed in the United States of America

For free catalog write:
Global Communications
P.O. Box 753
New Brunswick, NJ 08903

Free Subscription to Conspiracy Journal E-Mail Newsletter
www.conspiracyjournal.com

THE MASTER SYMBOL
OF
THE SOLAR CROSS

COMPILED BY TARVIS
WITH
CHANNELING BY TUELLA

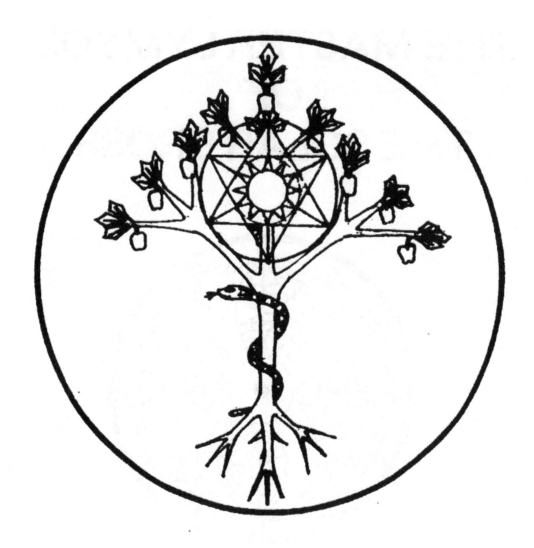

"No effort for the good of others is ever lost. Whether or not the person who planted its original seed, may see the fruit from that effort, it will remain. The results will ever continue, as a Tree of Life, as the fruit of its Knowledge becomes imperishable through the Understanding within the hearts of others."

THE MASTER SYMBOL
OF
THE SOLAR CROSS

Sponsored
By
The Great Brotherhood Of Light

Compiled
By
TARVIS

Channeling
By
TUELLA

DEDICATION

This book is dedicated to All who
search for Eternal Truth, that
through its application, they
can serve to bring about
THE COSMIC AGE.

THE MASTER SYMBOL
OF
THE SOLAR CROSS

Published 2008 by
Inner Light/Global
Communications

Timothy Green Beckley

ILLUSTRATIONS by TARVIS

•••

MUSICAL PATTERNS

by TUELLA

PREFACE

In the beginning we were made perfect, undifferentiated blanks, starting a 'Journey of Growth' which is the whole point of existence. Through innumerable personal experiences we evolve towards perfection of every aspect of our being. Every experience at any stage of development is equally important, and incomparably unique. The very process of Life is the product, and not necessarily the final result. Each aspect of Life is important in its own place; therefore, an overall balance and a holistic approach is essential to our complete growth. The Solar Cross ⊕ represents this process of Life.

The choice that each of us must make is either ongoing adaptation, or extinction. Adaptation is the ability to constantly transcend and widen our present narrow belief structure, to absorb many new diverse factors, and thus bring about a much higher civilized way of Life. Extinction is the ability to constantly ignore the true direction of growth, which is the purpose for Life, and to limit progress through base actions of ignorance.

The purpose of this book is to expose you to the various concepts, which will gradually awaken within you a desire for learning more about the Universe, our relationship to it, our purpose in Life, where we came from, and where we are going. You are free to believe or disbelieve the statements that are present in this text, but let each of you realize that your personal conclusion in no way alters THE FACT OF THEIR REALITY ⊕ .

TARVIS

FOREWORD

HATONN:

"Symbols began as a method of implanting profoundly essential concepts at the subconscious level of mind within all souls by the Creative Spirit, to be brought into consciousness later as they developed. The basic symbol of the Solar Cross ⊕ encompasses a very broad spectrum of awareness in its complete relativity to all things. As the Key of Unfoldment, the Solar Cross ⊕ will inwardly awaken many souls to both the vital and the valid approach of the Universal Science ⊕ of Life."

ALJANON:

"We present to you the timeless Master Symbol of the Solar Cross ⊛ , which represents the Universal Laws of Creation. These basic truths have been in existence for eons of time, as principles of creative evolution. At this point in time, there is that 'Remnant' of those now embodied who are capable of understanding and applying them. Therefore, once more they are given in a correct sequence to assist you in making total progress in all phases of Life."

MONKA:

"We of the Brotherhood of Light sponsor this book for the purpose of enlightenment ✹ . We request that these teachings be considered and shared with as many as is possible. We will observe whether or not they were effective in removing the memory blocks, so that recall can occur, depending upon individual efforts. In the Light of All of US, who must oversee the Awakening of the human race, through education, we work and strive together as a 'Team,' to that end."

✡

THE BROTHERHOOD OF LIGHT

CONTENTS

SECTION   PAGE

ONE   THE SOLAR CROSS   1

TWO   THE SOLAR TONGUE. 21

THREE   THE UNIVERSAL SCIENCE . . 41

FOUR   THE UNIVERSAL LAWS. . . . 59

    0. Central Force   77
    1. Life.   83
    2. Magnetic Resonance. . . .   89
    3. Action and Reaction . . .   95
    4. Vibration 101
    5. Light 107
    6. Mind 113
    7. Harmony 119
    8. Dimensions. 125
    9. Love. 131
   10. Polarity. 137
   11. Attraction. 143
   12. Manifestation 149

FIVE   THE MASTER SYMBOL 155

SIX   THE GREAT AWAKENING . . . 173

SEVEN   THE GREAT LESSON. 199

CONCLUSION. 236

ACKNOWLEDGEMENTS. 237

BIBLIOGRAPHY. 239

INDEX OF CONTACTS

NAME	TITLE	ORIGIN	NUMBER
Affa	Linguist	Uranus	1
Akasan	Cosmic Teacher	Venus	2
Aljanon	Creative Thought Master	11th Plane	3
Balinos	Universal Law	Semulus	4
Belshar	Galactic Tribunal Bootes	Arcturia	5
Cryxtan	Science Coordinator	Venus	6
Hilarion	Chohan of Science	12th Plane	7
Kalen-Li	Universal Master Korendor	Krystalina	8
Korton	Telepathic Coordinator	Mars	9
Kuthumi	World Teacher	12th Plane	10
Lattrob	Cosmic Teacher	Korendor	11
Lonzara	Cosmic Science Master	Venus	12
Monka (Kel-Ran)	Solar Tribunal Chairman	Mars	13
Sedat (Hatonn)	Universal Records Keeper	Terminus Hatonn	14
Soltec	Astrophysicist	Centuras	15
Zo	Physicist	Neptune	16

(The source and contact are identified by a letter and number to the left side of paragraphs. When not so indicated, it means that the compiler has made an enclosure within the text.)

THE MASTER SYMBOL
OF
THE SOLAR CROSS

COMPILED BY TARVIS
WITH
CHANNELING BY TUELLA

ONE

THE SOLAR CROSS

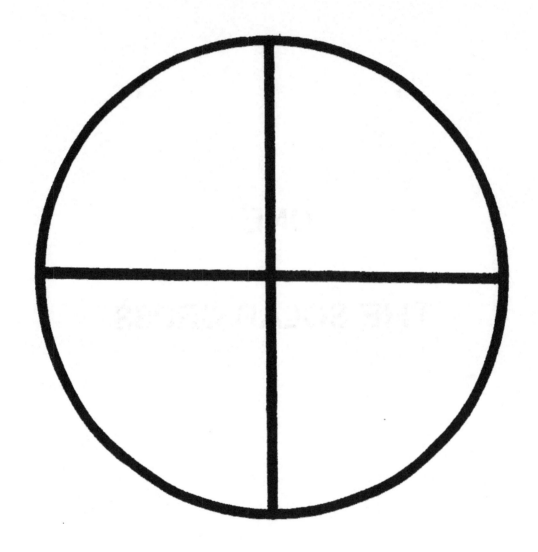

THE SOLAR CROSS

In the ancient history of the people of planet Terra, sacred symbols were used in teaching all the basic principles of nature. Everything was taught in the simplest, most comprehensive language of symbols, used as object lessons, that could be understood by anyone. All were taught in stages, where sight would supply the absence of spoken words. At every step the student was confronted with symbols of the omnipresent power and wisdom of the Creator ⊙ .

In the broadest sense, the Unnamable Creative Spirit has outlined the Evolutionary Plan of Creation, through the manifestation of the Universal Laws of Central Force ⊙ .

A   "The Purpose of Life throughout the Cosmos, and inherent within everyone, is the desire to rise to something higher ⋀ . Therefore, we were endowed with the ability to reason, that we may eventually know and understand all states of Creative Expression in the scheme of All Life."

In the Infinite Progress of All Life ⊕ , each ultimately will comprehend the many forms of Law expression, as governing forces.

Symbols were created from studying Natural Laws, which apply to every phase of existence, to serve as a guide for progress to the Source of All Life ⊕ .

When we discipline ourselves through choice, we evolve to a state of accomplished or completed oneness within the Creative Spirit. And when we refuse to work with the Cosmic Principles, we suffer the consequence of such choice. Life (Power), Light (Intelligence) and Love (Creation) must be as one, in unity, before any progress can be realized. The Solar Cross ⊕ is the master key which will unlock this phenomenon of the Universe. Life is Perpetual Motion, for Creation is ever constant. It is a growing and expanding Universe, within which we have our being.

Life is unending, manifesting, changing, aging, dying. It goes endlessly on ⊕ . Change is the manifestation of all, the Perpetual Motion of the Creator. God is an oscillating charge ∿ superimposed on an infinite point ⊙ , constantly causing a transformation of space, exerting its influence on the unmanifest, automatically creating energy + , and in consequence, matter ◯ .

God sent out the sparks of our spirit + , to experience and to serve ⊕ . There are hundreds of thousands of testing grounds in the Universe, of which planet Earth is a part, where beings evolve upwards on the Scale of Life. Upon our plane, we must serve out an evolutionary period before we can ascend to higher worlds. Our Life, to be complete, requires a lot of thoughts and experiences. The physical body ◯ through which our spirit intelligence + expresses, is part of the Plan to provide us with the necessary experiences. If we do not realize this Truth of

Creation, then we will return to the planet until we have learned the Great Lesson, by living in accordance with the Laws of the Plan.

The vertical line | represents the descent of Spirit, and the horizontal line — represents matter, thus forming a cross + , through which the Divine self endures conflict or pain in its effort to express in the physical dimension ⊕ . The cross is the symbol of purification through balance of forces + within the circle ◯ of existence. The Cross + of energy within the Circle ◯ of matter, combined, form the Circle-Cross ⊕ , to symbolize physical life.

Through the forming of the cross + , our spirit is enabled to manifest through matter ◯ , in Creation. And by balancing our positive | and negative — forces through the upliftment of the lower segment of the cross + in matter until the vertical equals the horizontal line ⊥ , we then become complete luminous beings ⊕ , thus entering into the fourth or etheric dimension of the Divine. The Cross of Light and the Circle of Love, *together as one symbol,* represent the eventual freedom and *ascension of the Soul* ⊕ . The symbol has a numerical value of three.

The Circle-Dot ⊙ is the symbol of the perfect being, and the Cross + is the symbol of the path to becoming one with the Creator, through the Ascent ⋀ of our soul ⊕ . In the material world and mortal consciousness of the illusion of Time, our present existence separates us from our eternal and perfect self.

Everything that comes into being is an aspect of Mind, the Spirit of the Creator ⬦ . God creates from the Mind by thought vibrations ⬙ and life essence ⊙ . Force and Intelligence create by changing the rate of vibration and wavelength; varying movements, patterns, forms and substances come into being. Upon these diverse changes are based the endless designs and divisions in force and matter for the whole constant pattern ⊕ . All matter moves and changes, assuming its design according to its own vibration and maintaining its activity by the pattern of attraction ⊖⊕ and repulsion ⊕ , the positive ⌐ and negative — poles of creative power ⊙ . Each design carries inherently within itself, its own plan of development ⊕ .

The material plane expresses the separation from Spirit, by our awareness. In the order of Creation, Divine thought expressed as Light, Love and At-One-Ment with all ≋ vibrations, as the Word. As a consequence, came All Images ⊕ of the Creative Spirit, and finally the Universe, wherein all evolve.

Evolution operates according to the free choice of each and every person. Creative spirits (Logos) ⊙ gave to us a will, so that we may have the power to choose and gain what we search for. We were created for a perfect part, to be free beings complete with wisdom, truth and power. So, in the whirl ⚡ of the many-sided conflicts which we must overcome within this plane, we ultimately attain the greater dimensions of existence.

The paths of finite life encompassing ◯ the physical plane are many and wide, but the paths of Eternal Life that ascend upward ⋀ to the spiritual plane are few and narrow. Once we cross ┼ the paths of self, for those of service we ascend to return no more. Life is a learning process, a path of action to reach the perfection of the Immortal Inner Self, whether in spirit or physical form. When all know and can realize their divinity or kinship with God and the true Reality, then all of our trials and errors will be over.

Spirit $+$ is the Real, and Physical $\bigcirc$ is the illusion. No person can enter into this realization until they have found the Life, Light and Love as One God (Logos) $\odot$ within their *own* Soul $\bigcirc$. The Logos is the Eternal Godhead of the Father-Mother-Child, the perfect Word, the Great Source $\odot$ which creates, destroys and saves, in Whom all have their Immortal Being $\oplus$. Love $\bigcirc$ is the power of this Creative Spirit that manifests   to all as the union that binds two souls $|$ — together in eternal oneness $\oplus$. When the Life, Light and Love are as one within our soul, there power, silence and speechlessness will rest, with the Radiant One $\odot$ in the center.

This attainment of complete education is necessary to form a closer relationship to the higher powers. An enduring relationship exists only when there are forces being exchanged $\oplus$ at many levels of being. Greater growth and development of the Whole Being is achieved only as this relationship also evolves.

Every soul is evolving into a state of self-consciousness wherein it at last recognizes its own divinity $\oplus$. The Cross $+$ of Light enfolding within the Circle $\bigcirc$ of Love is the Star of the Perfect Balance of Power $\oplus$. The Cross within the Circle is the symbol of self sacrifice and service to all God's family. We are made perfect, with feet firmly planted on the ground, arms equally outstretched in the form of the Cross in an attitude of service and blessing.

Source $\odot$ in Its Infinite Wisdom caused all Its creations to function by perpetual motion ⊕ . It maintains the balance by centering ⊙ each creation and insulating each one from all others as individual units ⊕ . The Creator remains neutral ⊕ , a division point between the contrasting poles of force. God is present everywhere, in an Eternal Universe. God is a line parallel to Itself and vibrating on Itself at right angles ♃ , exhibiting equal actions in all directions ⊕ . God is a system of axis with the intersection of the lines of force being Omnipresent; thus dimensions are contained within Him. When these are permutated to infinity ∞ , He is many. God acts as a transformer and creates energy ✛ and matter ◯ , thus perpetuating Himself as similar Life systems or units of God ⊕ .

The Solar Cross ⊕ is a Key of the Creative Plan of Evolution. The Circle-Cross ⊕ essentially symbolizes: a. The Creative Spirit; b. The Cosmic Powers; c. The Creation; and d. The Plan of Evolution.

*   *   *

a. THE CREATIVE SPIRIT

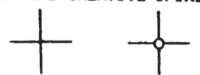

Four Forces from God

The Cross $+$, in one form or another, has always been the symbol of spiritual or unseen power. It is the symbol of the force of the opposite polarities. The circle ◯ signifies the circumference encompassing everything, the Creator. It is an endless line representing infinity ∞ , with no beginning and no ending. The sinewave ◐ passing through the circle represents the curved but finite positive | and negative — aspects of polarity which operate within the Infinite Universe ⊕ .

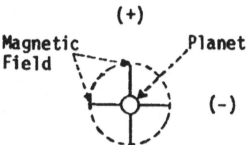

Planet in Balanced Magnetic Field

In this symbol, the circle of the planet is placed within the cross at the point of balance in the center, representing the planet operating within balanced forces. When the positive | or negative — pole is longer than the other, it is the symbol of imbalanced forces.

M16   "The Four Great Primary Forces are: Static Magnetic Field;Electro-Static;Electro-Magnetic Wave; Resonating Electro-Magnetic Field. We have a symbol for this in the Solex Mal.   It is similar to your so-called swastica ⊕ . The Four Forces coming out of the Creator. It is one of the most ancient of Saras (Earth) symbols. That is not strange. It is because the ancient people of your world understood nature and this knowledge has since been lost to you."

Space, Time and Energy are also manifestations ⊕ of Primary Light Force ⊙ . Each with an axis of existence, radiating from the very core or pivot ✛ , to direct the flow of secondary energies. In a planetary system about a sun, we have a vertical axis ❘ , a horizontal axis — in circular form ◯ , an equator, and a field axis • of resonating force ≋ which permeates all the atoms and molecules of Matter. We have three axes, two at right angles to one another ✛ and a third ◯ , within the organizer of the field itself, thus ⊕ .

Power is only manifested through an interchange or differential ⊕ between the positive and negative poles, creating motion ⊕ or ⊕ . Controlled power is that which is given to direction. Motion can exist only when there is an imbalance between two or more poles. That which is in balance cannot move of itself, without some other force causing the action. The Universe is kept in motion because of its imbalance seeking an equilibrium. Were it ever to attain a balance, all motion would cease. Every celestial body that rotates on a magnetic axis represents a balance of motion in the form of imbalance, which is constantly seeking an equilibrium.

When there is a precise interchange of Primary Light Energy through imbalanced opposites, only then does Life manifest itself ⊕ . All matter manifesting Life in balanced motion moves in an arc ⊖ , and in imbalanced motion in an angle ⊥ . Life is the carrier of development in endless spiral ⊕ Therefore, the stages are positive ⊕ and negative ⊕ or both ⊕ when they are in balance.

*   *   *

b. THE COSMIC POWERS

An equal lined Cross + symbolizes that it is through a balance of power that we gain control over matter ◯ . The Cross, with its lines radiating out from an inner or cen- ter Circle + , represents the Cosmic Powers innate in us. It is the symbol ⊙ which un- folds our co-creative attributes through our physical ⊕ form. In the Solar Tongue ☼ ∽ , they are known as the Creative T-EL-OS powers .

A   "The human body is composed of elements and minerals which serve us by obeying the energy impressions we place upon them. The state of our thoughts determines the expressions of our body. Without constantly serving the intelli- gence within the body, its atoms cannot rise to a higher state of expression. Therefore, we are both a product by molecules ◯ of planet Terra, and a product of our Divine Cre- ator + .

The physical ♀ part of our being has been endowed with four + channels of sensory per- ception: sight, hearing, taste, and smell, through which it expresses ⊕ . The intel- ligence ⊙ that precedes all other senses is touch, or in reality, the soul of the body, part of the All Inclusive Intelligence. Touch is the primary sense of the Life of the human body. Our body operates in a field of sensa- tion and feeling, independent of others, which is conscious consciousness.

The real intelligence which gives sensation to other four senses is a Universal One ⊙ . The intelligence is the eternal reality behind the temporary illusion of the physical body ⊙ . When this touch or life leaves the body, the other four senses have no power of sensation to be active ⊙ . When all of this is understood, the four channels of our being will begin to evolve to serving the Divine Intelligence as very sensitive and powerful tools for learning ⊕ ."

The Life Force from Spirit ⊙ quickens, reanimates our total being ⊕ , giving us the ability to express creative power and thereby perfect ourselves and the planet. Inanimate matter is third dimensional. Our body, which is expressing intelligence through soul and mind, is fourth dimensional. The brain, acting as an instrument of our mind, is only a receiver and transmitter of Life energy, to activate the various motions and expressions of the body. When we unblock our mind (seven centers) and let the spirit of God flow through it, then we can achieve all states of Mind + over Matter ○ , thus ⊕ .

H15 "Complete Sensory Perception (CSP) — assists us to *detect* objects, events and thoughts. Complete Sensory Kinesis (CSK) | enables us to *act* upon objects, events and thoughts.

Each of these fundamental traits (CSP and CSK) has a real existence in the Universe. These faculties detect and move everything in matter, energy, space and time. When both are used in sequence, they assist us in pursuing a single line of thought for any period of time. All is possible in the overlapping series of the dimensions or planes of thought.

From the two basic functions of CSP and CSK manifest all of the different secondary effects, such as Telesight, Telepathy, Teleportation, and Telekinesis, just as colors are different manifestations of Light ☼ or + ."

Ultraconscious ⊙ (UC), is the Solar

Sense, controlled directly by both the Conscious and the All-Mind. It is the Direct Link with the Universe, as the vehicle of all parapsychic abilities. The Four Cosmic TELOS Powers, in order and function, are:

Sensory Ability	Organ of Brain
1. Telesight, or Clairvoyance	A nerve connecting Pineal gland to brain from Pituitary gland.

Telesight is seeing at a distance, beyond the range of physical sense of sight, by Mind.

2. Telepathy	Pituitary and Pineal glands.

Telepathy is mind-to-mind resonance, transmitting and receiving thought at a distance.

3. Teleportation	A small bulb located between Rathke's pouch and Pituitary gland.

Teleportation is the dematerialization and rematerialization of the physical body from one point to any other desired point in space, by the All-Mind.

4. Telekinesis	Same as above (3).

Telekinesis is a power by which a Mind can control matter, change its form, move it, shatter it, assemble it, recreate, etc.

*   *   *

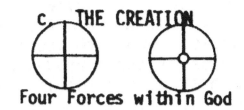

Four Forces within God

The Four Great Primary Forces are used to constantly Create, Develop, and Transform, through establishing a Vortex. From the Cosmic Mind (•) there flows forth vibrational waves of thought, which disperse through the ether and bring about the coalescence of minute particles. Protons | and electrons — are brought into proximity with one another and form the basic building blocks of Matter ⊕, from the atoms.

Polar Vents

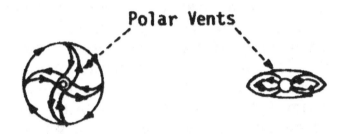

Top   and   Side
View of RMF surrounding a Nucleus.

L   " When positive | and negative — magnetic light lines of force cross + , both poles form a vortex . The whirlpool then condenses the positive particles into a nucleus, at three stages of evolutionary form: (1) A Proton of an Atom; (2) A Comet into a Planet; and (3) A Sun of a Solar System."

H15   " Space is filled almost to the saturation level with atoms attracting one another. These rays of influence upon the atoms brings them into close proximity with the very structure of each atom, to form a cooperative magnetic unit.

They begin to gather, forming whirlpools that spiral inward ⊘ , gradually tighter, and ever increasing in velocity. A blazing nebula of atoms exists, about to become molecules. The glowing mass in space produces radiation, which creates heat. As a result of heat, there is a chain reaction, and expansion occurs, which develops pressure.

The field of influence broadens; it is circular and spherical. Atoms are continually drawn through the spiral arms of the nebula into its innermost core ⊙ . In this cosmic whirlpool ⊘ , the forces of radiation, temperature and pressure make it possible to create ⊕ molecules, the secondary building blocks of Matter.

Molecules, upon being formed, attract one another, developing a larger whirlpool ⊘ . With the gathering of many molecules, more heat and light is produced, forming a white-hot glowing mass within the nova, a central sun. The new-formed sun goes through many cycles of change, growing hotter, until it blasts away its radiations into nearby space, cooling its surface, and it condenses ⊕ . Only in its very core ⊙ does tremendous heat exist. Then in the cycle of regeneration, external radiation begins to feed the eternal flames within the core. Expansion begins to occur, then heat is radiated off from its core, vaporizing or breaking up the condensed molecules, and returning them to the freer state of floating particles. The sun continues to expand until it blazes into a nova ⊙ ."

The Solar Cross ⊕ in each stage or condition represented "Accomplished Creation"; whether as an atom, molecule, sun or galactic system, it was a complete unit.

*   *   *

d. THE PLAN OF EVOLUTION

All evolves in a sequence, through proper
order and harmony in the Universe. Every movement of the stars and planets within this Cosmos has an effect upon all matter, energy,
space and time within it. This makes it possible for progress, growth and activity to occur in a procedure of balance. Outside of this
pattern, any development becomes strained and
difficult. The sequence of evolution which directly influences us, manifests in three parts
of one cycle:

1. We were created of a balanced Creative
Spirit $+$ which projected Itself into the
poles of positive (male) $|$ and negative
(female) $-$ vibrations of force. When we
recognize our own individual creation (spiritual), conscious mind (mental), and personality (physical), then we are enabled to unify
through these three forms of awareness $\oplus$.

2. Once this integration, attunement, and
alignment of our consciousness is completed,
we are then ready to unify with another. Our
two original beings in consciousness then
strive to meet at a center point $\odot$ or a balanced force field of proper operating life, and
rise in evolution. Each pole (gender) or manifestation balances the other expression $\oplus$,
on the opposite side of the scales of experience, in an androgynous state of oneness.

3. Then each soul function and faculty (bipolar unit) projected out of the mind of God,
must find its balance with all others. This
is where each soul, which is a cell within the
Being of God, must find its proportionate place
and be at peace and harmony with all others of
that body as God $\oplus$. All within the Creator constantly are attempting to maintain that

proper operation that creates an enjoyable and absolute perfect purpose.

Experience within matter, energy, space and time permits our spirit to integrate itself as a 'unit' ⊕ . Each dimension or plane of evolution as a collective whole, gives us impetus (when recognized) for further integration as a cooperative unit of force. Integration is our sense of unity and oneness with all Life ⊗ . It is an outward symbol ⊕ of the inward consciousness and understanding. There is a certain level of a unified state which we must reach before we are able to remain together without the assistance of a covering of some type for our spirit.

We live in a three-dimensional ▽ world of matter, an illusion we perceive with our physical eyes. The material body is but a part of an illusion; we really do not exist at all as we think we do. The body is but a three-dimension ≋ vibratory expression in the mind ◈ which the soul ⊙ uses for a brief period on this planet. Almost every person upon Terra is a prisoner of their body, while a few control their form and other matter by use of the mind ◈ .

Everything we create must originate as thought ≋ , which consists of vibratory reflections under control of the mind ◈ . Certain glands under the brain (Pineal, Pituitary, and other), are those centers used by the All-Mind ◈ to achieve control over Matter, Energy, Space, and Time. However, these glands are, in most cases, degenerated and underdeveloped, just as our body's muscles become lax in absence of proper exercise ≋ . Through meditation on the three different levels of the Mind ≋ —Ultra- Inter- and Sub-Conscious, in a sequence pattern of Symbols, Words, and

Tones, they can be properly stimulated and exercised, as a complete Endocrine ⊕ Group. The Universal Laws serve multiple purposes on the spiritual, social and physical levels of being, thus assuring that the Plan of Evolution is accomplished.

Whatever we think, we can do. We are not limited by our physical body's time field; we are in a timeless zone and those who are tuned in to it, are aware of all. Those that use this timeless zone are in both the physical third and fourth dimensional reflection of the mind, without being able to break completely with the third. They experience an awareness of something other than physical, yet are still conscious of the third dimension.

Those who know the Universal Laws governing the *relationship* between Energy and Matter ⊕ , possessing the means☼ or power to make them function at will ⊙ , are capable of manipulating all types of phenomena in direct relationship to their power ⊥ . Matter is really only one substance ⊙ , hydrogen, altered in different ways ≋ to create or transmute ▽ other substances.

The Solar Cross assists us in the achievement of a universal point of view based upon complete understanding of the concepts of Life.

★   ★   ★

NOTES

TWO

THE SOLAR TONGUE

THE SOLAR TONGUE

C11

" From the Infinite Source ⊙, all things began. The Creation of Reality ⊕ manifested when the two polarities ⌐ of God ⊙ were combined ✝ . Positive is a higher, invisible vibration △ , termed Spiritual. Negative — is a lower, visible vibration ▽ , termed Material. When each form was created , it had a symbol or picture of a certain vibration , not duplicated by any other existing reality ⊕ . Each vibration which was thought , set into motion a different level , to stand forever as that symbol of reality ⊕ .

When certain EL-ements ⊙ and vibrations were combined to create this reality ⊕ , the effects ▽ were varied. Examples are the conversion of matter □ , energy △ , space ✝ and time ○ , into plants , fish , animals , and human life forms. As each reality was subcreated and came into existence by the EL Spirits ⊙ of the Creator, it was recorded upon them ▽ , and all spirits leaving the Source . The symbol's individual vibrational level of reality ⊕ became a part of the Solar Tongue , because it was created from

the highest vibration stepped down and combined
to form ▽ realities of material existence.

The objective purpose for departing ⊕ , was
to attain ∧ character of wisdom and strength
✡ , then return to original substance ⊙
with the experience of reality ⊕ , found
through the freedom of individuality ≋ . This
would enhance all creation ☀ , and The Creator ⊙ would thereby become more glorified
△ through all creations ⊕ . When we
became divided individual and dimensional creatures ⊕ , from the Source ⊙ , we were
given freedom of character and free will to
choose and subcreate our own realities ⊕ .
Reality symbols ⊕ became more complex com-
posites, as they came into manifestation ▽ .
All was new to us when we entered into consciousness of self ⊕ and everything.

The Universal Language ☀—𝔢 of Creation
⊕ , was essential to each of our spirits as
a Sol-ution ⊙ to understand and control the
physical covering for the spirit body △ .
This was thereby given in our early learning
stages ◎ , as the Law ⊙ of Reality ⊕ .
The problem of dominion over material reality
became the Great Lesson in Life ✡ . Re-
creation is the eternal progression ⊕ of Creation ⊕ . The Solar Tongue ☀—𝔢 is therefore the Creative Word ⊕ , which consisted
of Thought | and Word — . Thought | is of
positive polarity predominance △ , as it is
a causal, or projective force. Word — is of
negative polarity predominance ▽ , as it is
an effect expression, or inductive force.
These two | — are both necessary in order to
manifest a result ⊕ .

Consciousness is the Light ☀ , and △
energy, functions through the Spirit, which is
the Intelligence. Everything one creates must

originate as Thought, which consists of vibratory   reflections   under   control   of   the
mind.   The brain is an instrument of the mind.
The soul, expressing in the body, communicates
its   desires to the   mind.   The mind sends out
thoughts through the brain. The brain converts
these electrical impulses into sensory activity and/or physical movement, as speech.   All
of our   communication is at the Thought   level
of energy.   Words,   either as   written   forms
(symbols), or   as   spoken   forms (sounds), are
expressions of Thought vibrations. The Spirit
uses   many   forms of energy to   interact   with
others.

L   "In the drawing (on page 22), we see   the
Solar Disc or Circle. Extending out from this
disc, from left to right, is a curved or curled
tongue.   Therefore, it is literally a tongue as
well as a language referring to a tongue.   In
the Solex Mal (Solar Tongue), this is   the
symbol for the All Seeing Eye, the   Light   of
Creation, the four pointed star stands for the
Four Great Primary Forces   of   Creation,   the
flower of twelve petals represents the   twelve
planets."

M1   "Oarhae retto! We speak the original   language. We call it the Mother or Solar Tongue,
the Solex Mal. People of Saras (Earth)   spoke
this Universal language long ago. Your   Holy
Book tells you the story of this. 'The   whole
Earth was of one language, and of one speech',
Gen. 11:01. Your linguists will tell you that
all languages appear to come from   a   common
language. They do not know what this language
is, however. It is closely related   to   the
most ancient languages on Saras and ante-dated
them. All men of other worlds speak this language. You are a divided people, and you speak
many tongues."

L   "The Solex Mal is a symbolic, pictographic
language. When reading it in written form,
one interprets symbols instead of reading
words. Therefore, a symbol will be understood
by all whether they have seen the particular
symbol before or not."

"At one time man on Earth lived in a Golden
Age, and spoke with angels. In Atlantis, Lemuria and before, Earth people were in constant
contact with beings from outer space. Through
evil, greed, and lust, the Golden Age passed
from the Earth and with it went the ability to
speak the Solex Mal. We will again speak this
language of angels, in the New Age now dawning."

During the periods of Triteria △ , Lemuria
⚚ , and Atlantis ♆ , people reacted to to
sounds that are not audible to our physical
ears. They could mentally pitch ≋ a thought
along certain frequencies, at a given destin-
ation and then translate it into specific type
form (image), or in any number of ways. Their
language ☼ ๑ was extremely discriminating
in ways that most could not understand, simply
because gradations in pitch, frequency, and
spacing were so precise and complicated. Consider for example, something very simple like
a drawing of a Solar Cross ⊕ . Most would
perceive it simply as a visual object—a wheel
—but these people were great synthesizers. A
line was not simply a visual line, but according to an almost infinite variety of distinctions and divisions, it would also represent
certain sounds that would be automatically
translated.

An observer ◁◉▷ could quickly decipher the
meaning of the sounds before translating the
visual image, if one desired. In what would

appear to be a drawing of a wheel, for example, a Solar Cross ⊕ , then, the entire history or background of the ⊕ might also be given. Curves, angles, lines all represented, besides their obvious objective function in a drawing, a highly complicated series of variations in pitch, tone and value; as invisible words. Distances between lines were translated as sound pauses, and sometimes also as lengths of movement in time.

Color was used in terms of language in communication, and in art forms; representing somewhat, emotional graduations. The value or intensity of the color served to further refine and define, for example, either by reinforcing the message already given by the objective value of the lines, angles, and curves; or by modifying these in any given number of ways. The size of such symbols also spoke its own message.

In one way this was a highly stylized art, yet it allowed for both a high degree of preciseness of expression in terms of detail, freedom and scope. It was obviously highly compressed. The communicative and creative abilities were more vital, alive, and responsive than ours, because of this language system ☼⤶ . When we hear a word, we may be aware of a corresponding image ⊕ in our mind. With these people, however, sounds instantly built up an amazingly vivid image that was internalized, both multisensual and dimensional in character.

This technique was no longer used after the passing of the civilization of Atlantis. Today some of the remnants of symbols still exist in Tibet and South America. The keys to interpretation have been completely lost, except in a few instances. All that most would see is a symbol devoid of the multiple elements of meaning that gave it such great variety. It exists, herein, but would require individual reorientation to bring it alive.

There was an easy distinction between inner and outer sight, because certain sounds were used to indicate precise distinctions in terms of size, shape, direction, and duration, both in space and time. It was quite natural for them to close their eyes when in conversation in order to communicate more clearly, enjoying the ever-changing inner images that accompanied any verbal interchange. Education was an exciting and quick process of learning for them. Because this facility automatically produced brilliant pictures through using many sense channels simultaneously, much information could be impressed upon them.

Communication is the exchange of energy in a method to improve all relationships. The level of the relationship depends upon the level of communication. We must be consciously involved in the exchange. Good listening is hearing the words, focusing on their meaning, and discerning the tone energy. Open sharing and listening invites supportive and enduring relationships. We can be conscious and involved, or unconscious and separate. Energy can be projected to produce either positive or negative resulting reactions in others. The choice is ours to make.

Our knowledge of every aspect of existence is acquired and has results in one of two ways. We receive it either by experience or by conveyance of meaning from others, and apply this information either by placing it in storage to be recalled on demand, or by understanding it. Language is based upon perception, which is the recognition of general truths, and the reproduction of them, in a way which will awaken the same meaning in other perceptions.

There is a great difference between memory storage and understanding. In memory storage, bits of knowledge can be used only one by one, or in combinations which have been established. It is usable only in the precise form in which it was put into storage, with any change to it producing a certain amount of error. In understanding, it is usable in any form required, and in any combination with other facts which are understood. It is quite useful because it permits use in all sorts of permutations and combinations.

Understanding, or for any knowledge to have meaning, requires four things:

1. It must actually reach us accurately, either through our physical senses, or by direct mind contact, both of which are subject to distortions.

2. It must have its own significance to us. We must be coded to receive the meaning.

3. We must be able to process the fact, which is the fitting of it together until it becomes an integrated whole, self-consistent and meaningful.

4. We must cross reference the meaning with others who have been exposed to the same information, to verify its accuracy. This is not necessarily an easy thing to do.

The Solar Tongue is based upon a working understanding of the Universal Laws . Music (Harmony), Arithmetic (System), and Geometry (Balance), are the three primary components of this Creative Word. We were created to become synthesizing generator and distributor units of power existing in the body of God ⊙ . The keys to understanding the Cosmic Principles is contained in their Tone, Number, and Symbol patterns. The Source ⊙ by Plan, made the Laws of Nature to maintain the constant process of Creation ⊕ of the whole. The study of words is a conscious activity, the study of symbols *is a subconscious activity*. Certain fundamental laws do govern the flow ≋ of spiritual energy and determine the result of individual conscious or unconscious creative efforts ⊕ .

All of the Laws are built on creative thought, for All is Mind. We can use the Law to subcreate Reality ⊕ , through interaction ┼ of Thought and Word. Every single thing in the Universe exists solely because some intelligent being has, either consciously or unconsciously, brought it into being by use of the creative powers of thought. Creative thought waves, when properly concentrated and directed, can control the infinite energy flows of the Universe. Thus human mind can create ⊕ and destroy ⊕ . Thought is an all-powerful force which must be understood before it is employed to create or destroy. Belief and concentration must be *complete* : To the absolute exclusion of any and all other thoughts to consciously create ⊕ .

Telekinesis is a power by which a Mind can control matter, energy, space and time either outside or inside of its field of intelligence, up to a specific point. It is the 'Word-Power' ☼ ☞ , to act over material substance by means of using vibrational sound symbols as a transmutant and regulating force, to produce, control, or destroy elements at will. In this condition, the All-Mind is the go-between, the individual mind and the creative thought, or object, both of which compose it.

The cross ✛ is the symbol of the differential power between the positive (thought) and negative (word) lines of primary light ⊙ energy. By phasing ⊕ this interchange, unlimited power through motion is the result. When the power exceeds the differential phase, disintegration will result. Spiritual △ power that is unseen can only be understood when it is manifest in the Material ▽ effect that is seen, in combination ✡ , as directed by Mind ⊚ .

The first energy born from the original creation was the thought of Spirit Force, created by the high concentration of thought 'energy,' then into four forces. Through lowering its high vibration, thought changed to the material substance of 'matter.' Primary energy │ and matter — are equivalent in conversion ⊕ , as they are only existing in different vibrations, energy having a higher vibration △ , and matter, a lower vibration ▽ . Through this variation in energy, the elementary 'building blocks' of matter—the protons, neutrons, and electrons—were generated. From these parts of matter the atoms and molecules were built, which resulted in the creation of all chemical combinations. Some of these make up the stable ⊕ cells of the human body.

All Creation is self-contained and sustained within thought-form ⊕ , as an aspect of Infinite Force ⊙ , within Mind ⊚ , expressing in being within Itself. Creation is the result of the Laws of Cause (Thought) and Effect (Word).

The Solar Tongue  consists primarily of both Telepathic (Thought) and Verbal (Word) interchange ⊕ . Therefore, we will cover some basic facts concerning both, taking into consideration that they cooperate as one unit.

Thought

Color   Pattern

Telepathy is mind to mind resonance, or receiving and transmitting thoughts at a distance. The pituitary gland is the negative — contact point within the brain that enables us to receive the thought waves of others from any distant point. The pineal gland is the positive contact point within the brain that enables us to transmit our thought waves to others to any distant point.

The mind is a form of energy with a set frequency , different from any other. While this frequency cannot be changed, it can be phase synchronized to a Universal Frequency, which can be tuned to, opening the contact. When the mind is generating this frequency, it can transmit or receive thought impulses. The mind can select from any of these at will, and impose a mental block to shut out all others. When the frequency is not generated, no thought interchange will occur.

Telesight, or Clairvoyance, is the reception and transmission of visual images, or the tuning of sight beyond its physical range, at a distance. Thought pictures or colors are received or transmitted through a nerve connecting the pineal gland to the brain from the pituitary — gland. The Conscious Mind through the Ultraconscious tunes for the desired results.

Any field of Life vibration, such as

thought or aura waves, consists of various em-
anations that form a distinct pattern of colors. The inner portion of the energy impulses,
as a field of colors characterizes basic 'vibrational factors' of health power levels,
moral values, orientations, attitudes and moti-
vation. The outer portion emanates surface
emotions, conditions and preoccupations. The
overall pattern of colors indicates the evolution of an individual, or a thought concept,
as a sequence of events.

Word

⌐ϱ

Sound   Symbol

Language is composed of a root system of
symbolic speech. The positive | vowels (open
vocal sounds) and the negative —— consonants
(closed vocal sounds), are not easily spoken
without balance and force of the vowel. They
were basic harmony and balance in speech as
well as principle.   It was comprised of certain syllables to attune perfectly to the cosmic forces. Because of the higher frequency
and different harmonics in the tonal scale, it
would be unintelligible to us. The sound scale
is 15 octaves in length, with hundreds of tones.
For every semi-tone there are 6 myria-tones,
with the slightest degree of difference between
each minute tone.

Sound, color, and vibration of a high frequency (5 mm), can be used to project and receive a mental capsulation, or symbol, that can
release thought patterns in the subconscious
mind. Our brain converts experiences into symbolic meaning, as terms with some degree of understanding, because we are trained to speak.
All the input of our physical senses is channeled through the brain, as a composite symbol.

L   "Our linguists tell us that all languages appear to come from one common language, but they do not know what it is." Each version of language was constructed within the horizon of the race or group using that version. A short time ago, present-day English was Anglo-Saxon, a German dialect. Not very long before that, this was a Gaul (Roman), or Gael dialect. Gaelic was a late Scythian dialect of the order Euskara language, a branch of the Karian, Khami, and Tur language. This had grown out of ancient Sanskrit (Tibet). This 'root' language was the product of vowels and consonants which originated in a language of symbolic speech ☀⤳.

From the source of • One Life, ◯ One Existence, and ⊕ One Cause, the entire symbology was predicated. Speech, as the pure 'image' of Truth, expresses the two portions of Effect, the image of Cause, or Truth. Cause ⊙ 'spoke' Effects ╀ which produced a series of twelve results that systematically repeated themselves from the beginning to the final condition. 'Sound' was used to indicate that Cause ⊙ and Effect ╀ is the property of polarized force ⊕ , as sound, color and whirling vortex or circular motion.

From the geometrical symbols, numerals, and letters as roots of speech grew all written records. By the time the next era had reached the peak of their time in Lemuria, those roots and symbolic speech had begun to flourish as a language. Much of the original root symbols became ancient Sanskrit as a working basis, the trunk of the Tree of Language, so to speak.

The development of writing occurred in three stages:

a. Pictographs are pictures or symbols representing the object or *thing* shown. Pictographs can be readily *understood* without reference to syllabic sounds or words. Included are Ideagraphs, which are pictures representing the underlying *idea* associated with specific or general things. Both are interconnected, thus producing Logographs, or word picture writings (idea things).

b. Syllabic Words consist of a vowel sound or the combination of several, and one or more consonants. Syllables or words can be readily *felt* without reference to pictographs, or picture writing. A syllable system of writing requires the use of complex groups of consonants and signs for the purpose of combining them into words.

c. Alphabet was the link formed by combining Pictographs and Syllables into arbitrary letters. Alphabet consists of 24 signs, each standing for a single vowel or consonant (a,e,i,o, and u). A vowel is made mostly with the open mouth, and for a consonant, the tongue, lips and teeth must work variably together.

It was then recognized that pictographs, syllabic words, and letters could convey three independent meanings, or thoughts, emotions, and concepts. The fundamental divine intergalactic language  is a meaning conversion system of thought pictures into color, tone, and symbols, which formed the archetypes of the original word concepts. It is important to note that the Solar Tongue  was Trilinguia  , or threefold language. This means that we are capable of communicating in three phases: with God (Spiritual), any being

(Social), and animate form (Material), as one language, at various levels of expression. Each letter of the alphabet retains a conceptual meaning as well as a phonetic one. Learning this alphabet gives us the ability to assemble each symbol into a system of patterns which in turn convey pictures into conceptual information by following certain basic rules of syntax and assembly.

I   Here is the "Solar Alphabet" 🜨 , with associated concept meanings.

SYMBOL	CONCEPT
	Absorption, unity with God, or Awareness of Creative Spirit.
	BE, Being, to exist, or Bal-ance. BAR, Barraga, Brother, and BEN, good.
	CON, Conscience, to understand Change. Chea, or child.
	DR, Disintegrant Radiation, or DEK, Fire.
	EM, Emergence, or EN, Energy of all pervading motion.
	FE, Fecund, as in fe-male, Field of Force.
	GEN, Generate, or Gal, as wheel of forces.
	HU, Polarized constructing condition, or struggle of forces. Hae, or speak
	I-mage in action, conscious self, or Intelligence.

SYMBOL	CONCEPT
M	
•⟨	Kinetic, force of motion, D or T. "Karas, or contact."
∴	Life, the result of action and reaction. Lanka, or Light bringer.
⌢•	MAL, Negative Tongue. Max, or eye. Man, or human.
⫽•	NAS, instrumental, or seed.
⋁•	OS, Oscillation, vortex of force. "Saras, repetition."
⚥	PO, Power, achieved through Polarity predominance, or Progression. Patri, father.
⊣+	RA, dangerous quantity of disintegrant force in object. Retto, original.
⋔:	SOL, Solar, radiant energy given off through Shift of D and T phase motion.
⚱•	TE, Integration, the integrative force of growth, or Tese, interchange of two forces.
⊣⊦	UN, Universe, or Unit of Conscious Force.
⌣•	VA, Vasu, Love to another or vital magnetic force. Vec, space.
⅄	WA, Wan, Primary Light Force, Wan-4, the Four Forces (Will of Source).

SYMBOL	CONCEPT
·)⊖(·	Ex, Conflict, lines of force crossing one another. Cross mating of Adamic and Evas races.
¢|:	YO, Yonto, we are one in spirit, though we be two in matter.
)·⌐ ○	Za, a quantity of T energy neutralized by an equal quantity of D. Zabek, school of struggles.

Most of us are not aware that all the confusion between nations on our planet is only in the tongue ___☉, and not in our thinking ☼ . The 'Language Barriers' would be nonexistent were one tongue spoken. In one generation the people of Earth could communicate with one another, were a united decision made by each country, that on a certain date, all children born from that day forward would be taught the same language. Were this planetary language the Solar Tongue ☼ ☉ , then we could also communicate with those of many worlds throughout the Universe. It would serve as a root system for the translation of all tongues.

It is unfortunate, though, that those opposed to such a change (which was once attempted), also believe it is worth money not to understand each other, because we can continue to have conflicts for profit. A person should be made aware of their thought patterns and natural interests, with consideration for others, which is the basic function of having one language—to remove any obstacles in our relationship with all other beings.

The one consistent method of accurate com-

munication through the ages upon Terra has
been 'symbols,' which meant the same thing no
matter what the spoken languages or numeral
systems. We were originally given the Solar
Tongue ☀⟲ as a system of understanding
the Universe, so that we might bring our life
out of Chaos and into Cosmos. We could, were
our potential fully realized, accomplish anything. Only the limitation of our awareness
of reality ⊕ prevents us from attaining
this ability, and the Solar Tongue ☀⟲ is
the means of comprehending and utilizing this
Link ⊕ .

★   ★   ★

NOTES

THREE

THE UNIVERSAL SCIENCE

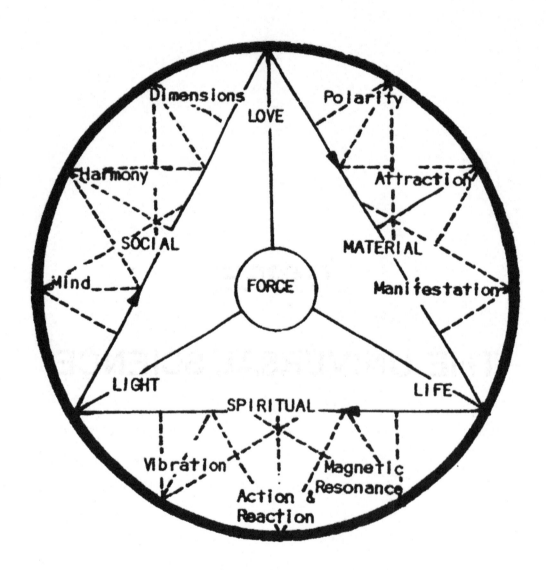

Cycle of Equal Development

THE UNIVERSAL SCIENCE

Universal Science is the whole without exception, of observed, verified and classified knowledge into a system, involving every aspect of existence. It is the philosophy of an understanding of all the phases of being, and the relationships which exist between all ultimate causes and effects in the Cosmos. Each phase is an interval in the process of complete development. In every life form there is a natural sequence of changes which recur as parts in one cycle of progress.

When applied to any particular part of existence, the Universal Science denotes the collection of Fundamental Laws under which all the subordinate activities related to that part are comprised. These basic principles form the relationship by which all operates in the Universe. With these object lessons as the foundation of education, all are able to learn very rapidly the full scope and purpose of Life.

The Complete Awareness of Being is the making of our perception of self whole in its relationship with everything. Reality is the totality of actual things, and only in a state of perfect unity can the Truth be made known. Our own conscious knowledge of the Real is relative to an understanding of the Universal Laws.

The three Primary Phases of Total Being consist of our relationship to, and study of: (1) the Creator, Spiritual (Life); (2) our fellow beings, Social (Light); and (3) the needs of the body, which include the supporting environment Material (Love). Each of these interdependent links must be developed with equal and constant effort for everyone to achieve complete awareness. This is also essential to our continued ability to adapt, cooperate, survive, and progress as a whole.

A   "Growth and development turned to a common good instead of individual benefit, always results in a state of perfection in all phases of life. When one particular phase is allowed to evolve as thought, without considering its effect upon the others, or its control, then it will ultimately bring about division and destruction to all concerned. It is the responsibility of everyone in the Universe to live in accordance with the Cosmic Principles, so that they can progress and accomplish many things. To defy them would result in eventual annihilation and delay of evolution."

The immortal spirit or higher self within our body is reached when the Primary Principles of Life (Power), Light (Intelligence), and Love (Balance) are blended in our consciousness as one unit. The God-Head of Source is a perfect blend, a balanced Trinity of Integration. We will evolve in terms of our inner being, and eventually return to the Source from which we came, as perfected beings.

The Symbol of Universal Science is a combination of a circle surrounding a triangle with three divisions and a circle in the center.

Symbol	Color	Principle
Center Circle	White	Source of All Force
Primary Triangle	Blue	Life or God Will
	Yellow	Light or Intelligence
	Red	Love

The three segments in the triangle signify the primary principles by means of which the whole celestial Universe is operated. These are the important keys to our divine powers. By interblending and balancing the three primary principles, nine other secondary principles result.

Secondary	Blue-Green	Magnetic Resonance
	Orange-Yellow	Mind
	Red-Purple	Polarity
	Green	Action & Reaction
	Orange	Harmony
	Purple	Attraction
	Green-Yellow	Vibration
	Red-Orange	Dimensions
	Purple-Blue	Manifestation

When we live, move and act in conscious awareness of Life, Light, and Love, we are keeping our complete being in divine and perfect order, as signified by the Source.

The symbol of the triangle △ within the circle ◯ forms the composite image of the concept of Creative Spirit ⊙ . The Three Primary Phases of Being, ⟁ within the Creator, cooperate in unity of purpose, so that all evolution is constant and immutable.

The Levels of Progress within which we can achieve control and self reliance as a Complete Being, are:

Level	Achieve Control
1. Physical	When we do not permit any desire to dominate us.
2. Consciousness	When we can use the brain to think and work out any problem.
3. Knowledge	When we can accumulate facts of information which are usable.
4. Wisdom	When we can apply these facts to select, plan and accomplish a goal.
5. Understanding	When we can receive and comprehend information which someone conveys.
6. Awareness	When we can use the mind as a link to the inner being and the Creator.
7. Telekinesis	When we can use the Creative Mind to change something by Universal Law.

PHASE I

The Spiritual relationship between our self and the Creative Spirit which pervades and controls the Universe is the Primary Principle of Life, or God Will. This part of development consists of the following Secondary Principles and Subjects of study:

a. Magnetic Resonance - Thought Force. Metaphysics is the study of the causes behind all mental activity beyond the five physical senses.

b. Action and Reaction - out of the center of Cause, is Creative Thought in Action, and effect is the Creation that follows. Theology is the study of the relationship between God and the created.

c. Vibration is the index of consciousness, the part of being which indicates our relationship to the original concept. Religion is the study of the belief in an anthropomorphic Deity, of a cause (Etiology).

Through our research into the manifestations of the Infinite Power and Intelligence, the Cosmic Plan of Evolution for Creation can be used to lift many aspects of our personal behavior out of the realm of Theology and Abstract Ethics, and into the area of practical use. The Source of Life is an Eternal Creative Spirit. Everything is surrounded and supported by One Power that gives it Immortal Life. Life does not belong to us. Were we to dissociate ourselves from God, we would die spiritually. Spirit is Universal Energy. Self consciousness divides us from our Source of Energy.

Spiritual consciousness is the relationship of our awareness to the Source and all expressions of Spirit. God is Unlimited, Infinite, expressing in all forms, as some degree of intelligence.

God is the Unmanifest, and those of us that are Created Spirits are in some degree manifest. The Cosmic Power, or Creator, is the generator of spirit-energy, different in form from that found in matter. A spirit can create to a certain extent, within limits, alter space, create and destroy. God is Unlimited in Power, able to create matter, energy, space and time. In addition, the Father is the only one who can create spirit, and other sources of Life, with power to alter space, similar to His own ability. The El-o-him Beings constitute, with Him, a single unit, in Themselves Eternal.

The Infinite Creator has various names: God, Radiant One, Unnamable, and is without gender, being Eternal. The Creative Spirit is not given to one polarity alone, but expresses all. God is Unmanifest, as such, Infinite; within are all manifestations or dimensions contained. As spirit, we are an eternal part of the totality of Creation in all things, both responsible for and responsive to, it. All spirits were created by the same Infinite Being; therefore, all are equals and should be acknowledged as such, in every interaction.

Spiritual growth is the universal desire for freedom, liberty and worship of One Creator, along with equality for all. Spirituality within us consists of the concept and understanding of the Laws or principles of the Universe. It is the outworking of them, as cause and effect, our contribution to All. When we live according to the Laws of God, our living becomes a testimonial of our worship, so there is no need for church edifices.

A   " When we are aware of our true inner being, and abide in the cosmic unit of Creative Life, Light and Love, we are happy and progress rapidly. The soul can build the physical body, and enable it to grow and express divinity. Our Cosmic gifts are inherently known as we blend or evolve to the level of the Complete Being within us."

In order to gain true life, we must lose the aspect of self, which is only for self, and become aware of our personal identity in service to all the Universe. Each person has a spiritual, or unknown self which transcends the material world and consciousness, dwelling eternally out of the Time dimension in perfection. It is our spiritual purpose to attain reunion with our immortal consciousness, made in the Image and likeness of God. We are both mortals and potential gods.

One can only know God by reaching Him as Idea—not physically. Every soul goes through at least one hundred thousand life tracks as it returns toward God. All, since their creation $\oplus$ as conscious beings, were given the ability of awareness to understand the Creative Spirit, within themselves. All have the spirit or creative force.

At one time in our original creation in the Image of the Spirit of God, we were an atom, and then by going through a pattern of evolutionary processes, we expanded that structure to that which we are today. Each experience was recorded by eons of living, and we evolve to a point where we are in His Image and have the ability to re-create. Re-creation is a privilege only given to those who have conformed to the Cosmic Laws. One can descend in this pattern of growth and development until they no longer have the ability to re-create.

As a result, everything then becomes opposite to the creation, and they actually cause destruction instead of re-creation.

Everyone, in their natural mental state, aligns themselves with the Universal Laws, either consciously or unconsciously. Spirit energy of which we are composed is the substance of the Universe, and is manipulated and manifested through the processes of Cosmic Law. The Universal Laws are the means for accepting complete responsibility for the Reality We Create, and can be used to reshape it.

*   *   *

PHASE II

The Social relationship between our self and any other person or life form is the Primary Principle of Light, or Intelligence. This part of development consists of the following Secondary Principles and Subjects of study:

a. Mind is neutral and directs the flow and action of thought energy. Sociology is the study of the progress and structure of a group of intelligent beings bound together by common interests and standards to achieve specific results.

b. Harmony is order and balance of being. Government is the study of the rules disseminated and exercised through an organized body of individuals, to regulate the conduct of the whole, to protect the existence of both.

c. Dimensions are successive planes of conscious intelligence, and levels of progress. Parapsychology is the study of the motivations of beings as they live and interact with one another on different planes of existence.

We are gathered together upon this planet and density to blend as one, in harmony and tolerance, to bring about cooperation as a whole. Life should be a voluntary association of persons working together for the welfare of all inhabitants. A state of unity among everyone will create and maintain a bond of equality in every relationship, motivated through a desire for constant progress. Our existence is interdependent upon the ability of all others to mutually coexist.

Cooperative living means caring for one another and being concerned. A cooperative group of individuals combining their efforts can provide a better environment for living and achieve greater companionship. All human beings on this planet, regardless of race, color, creed, or sex, are members of one family, as one being. When we live a highly ethical life, both inwardly and outwardly, treating every other human being as our brother or sister, every prejudice is conquered. After living these beliefs for several years, every aspect of life, as a whole, takes on a greater meaning, responsibility and reward. To be selfless requires being compassionate, which overcomes human dislikes; thus, we become more fair and equitable in our activities with others.

Discipline of selfless service and obedience to the purpose of greater cooperation, makes it possible for every member of the organized group to be more directed in their growth and evolution as a unit. Every participant of the group must be committed to working towards what is best for the whole, including its goals, or it will eventually scatter its usefulness.

When people understand one another they are tolerant, cooperative, and interested in mutual progress. To understand another individual requires the ability of one to put himself in the other person's situation and be aware of those things which concern him. The needs, desires, hopes and fears of all people are essentially identical on our planet. Our existence is, for all purposes, dependent upon the well-being and mutual cooperation of other people, because all exist and provide in some manner for the whole world.

A   "When we permit our personal emotions to take control and separate us from an awareness of that eternal part of our self, judgments enter and divisions are established. The person of limited understanding projects thoughts into actions which contain discriminations, divisions, judgments, and personal feelings. We should understand our thoughts and their effects upon us as well as others, turning our minds toward the source of these thoughts and the reasons we allow them to control us. We should be the masters of our thoughts, yet not many of us are, because we do not understand ourselves. Nor have we taken the time to gain such understanding."

All Creation responds together as One. All intelligent beings, on all planets and dimensions of space, are to be regarded as brothers, regardless of race or physical form, if any, and whether or not they may at times be erring, must be treated as such. We must see value in each one we contact, exactly as we perceive worth within ourself. It is essential always that all work and strive together with open minds, ever aware that all is never known. Just as there are many upward paths leading toward progress, so there are those that guide downward into destruction. Though one may choose one path, and a second choose another, this need not divide them, as one may learn much from the other, if he will. Progress makes all brothers or sisters tolerant toward another's effort, even though it may be different from their own.

One can attract character, understanding, and Love by association with those who express these attributes through their actions. All people should live Universal Law and Love everyone, to live in peace and work together, because life is eternal.

The dividing line between help and interference is very delicate, and sometimes difficult to perceive. It is a mark of individual and collective progress to be guided by this

distinction. Certain sequences of experiences
are very necessary to each person's development and must not be altered significantly,
without considering the consequences.   Our
present deplorable world state is directly at-
tributable to the violation of this principle.

*   *   *

PHASE III

The Material relationship between our self and the needs of the body, which includes the supporting environment, is the Primary Principle of Love. This part of development consists of the following Secondary Principles and Subjects of study:

a. Polarity is created, maintained and transformed by the union of positive and negative poles of force. Physics is the study of the relative activity of matter, energy, space, and time.

b. Attraction is the force of unlike poles pulling together, as they seek balance. Health is the study of the maintenance of balance in the human body and its energy field, and Ecology within the planet.

c. Manifestation is creation through the action of thought force. Industry is the study of the manufacturing of those products essential to the continuance of physical life as a whole.

K2 "Our planet has the ability to abundantly supply all things to meet all the needs and reasonable desires of our people for many generations to come, were things intelligently produced and fairly distributed. Peace can only be achieved when the economic factors of energy to produce the essentials of Life are met. We have been given an unlimited balanced source of magnetic energy to draw upon. This free energy is made available by tapping the resonating field formed by the interaction of the sun and planetary radiation. With the application of these factors, we can simply agree to get along with each other, and dispose of our weapons of destruction."

When we observe the physical and chemical
Laws of the Material plane to which our bodies
are subject, health is maintained. By oppos-
ing these, Life is unhealthy, often to the
point of collapse. The balance of health must
be maintained and developed in Conscious Awareness along specific lines. There are many facets to the magnetic energy frequencies in the
operation of a body. The action, reaction and
interaction, plus the individuality of our energy frequencies, all influence the pattern of
health or ill health.

E   "The atmosphere we live within is composed of
gases and energy. All forms of Life substance
result from the unlimited combination of energy
frequencies acting on these gases. Each has
its own individual energy vibration to establish and maintain Life, Growth, and Development. So long as this magnetic energy is established and flows through without obstruc-
tion, we are in tune with the energy source
that runs the entire Universe."

"The physical characteristics of the body
occur at conception, while the individuality
is determined at birth. This action represents the influence exerted by the Trinity of
Suns, which are a part of God Force or Forces
   , that combine different energy frequencies as one, to establish and regulate the magnetic Life field."

The human ray energy is conducted, transmitted, and activated by the energy currents
in the body, organically constructed for this
812 purpose. "The Life Force enters into our whole
being by Four Essential Functions:

    a. *Thought* (Mind) is the inflow of Spiri-
tual Insight and ideas which we need in order
to wisely control our physical power.

b. *Motion* is acting promptly upon constructive new ideas.

c. *Breath* is the inflow of vital electrical currents from the air.

d. *Food* is the needed chemical elements which the physical body requires in order to conduct the vital Life energy throughout effectively.

Health consists of the balanced equal development of these vital expressions. To place emphasis on any one function and ignore the other three is a serious error."

E   "In the lower abdomen is the master brain, an intricate system forming the magnetic field. It is the grouping together of the main trunk nerves with their branches and relay networks extending throughout the entire body. In a normal state, the magnetic field gives the lungs the strength to pull in all of the energies. The magnetic field energy drawn from the air through breathing supplies the subsidiary brain, all organs, and relay centers of the entire body."

"The human ray energy has its origin in a portion of the Trinity of Magnetism, and this power of powers is composed of three sun systems of energy. There are three human rays, that are divided into twelve magnetic frequencies each for the entire body. Distribution of this energy field begins at the master brain or solar plexus. From this center Life energy is sent to the subsidiary brain within the skull for producing motor impulses to the body. This energy action and reaction on all centers of intelligence for the body is Life."

"From birth to adolescence the body receives

nerve power by radiation, from others. There-
after, for continued proper functioning, the
nervous system requires a greater supply of its
own energy, plus a mating energy. This recharging normally takes place during the relationship of sex with a person having properly
mated energies. The nervous system is constantly influenced by the energy from all human
contacts throughout Life. The Trinity of Magnetic Energy consists of three poles:

a. Positive recharging energy is generated
between persons born in the same sun sign, but
in a different month, through interaction.

b. Neutral nullifying energy is generated
between persons born in the same sun sign and
month, through interaction.

c. Negative discharging energy is generated
between persons born in the opposite sun sign
and month through interaction."

The Universal Science is a pattern of concepts, all intended to indicate the existence
of certain Natural Laws. Any concept, to survive, must be provable.

★   ★   ★

FOUR

THE UNIVERSAL LAWS

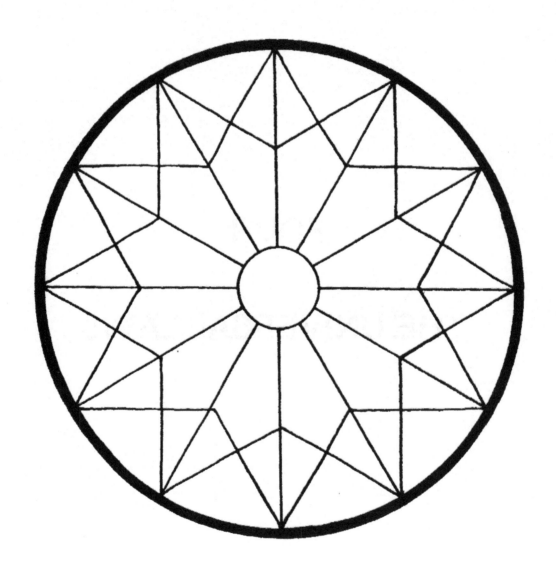

THE UNIVERSAL LAWS

The Creative Spirit accomplishes all purposes by the Universal Laws. Nature was created and built upon Fundamental Laws. These Laws of Creation were in the beginning, and will endure throughout eternity. They will reveal, through simple reasoning, all the operating principles of nature. Understanding of these Laws, as principles, both uplifts and restricts, because as we grow in experience of them, we will develop a greater regard for The creative actions and reactions of our thoughts towards our basic oneness, or relationship with All Life.

The inherited abilities of the Creator are embodied within its Creation. But its Creation must use the same consciousness which the Creator projected the Creation. This is where we, of a Cosmic Cause, must learn the consciousness of that Cause, of Central Force. The consciousness of the Creator, which we label Christ, is the Cosmic Consciousness of All, embodied into one. The Radiant One is the consciousness of All Life. The Universal Laws were released to assist us towards the advancement of the Cosmic Consciousness.

The philosophy of the Laws of the Universe

is based upon the understanding and the acceptance of the existence of a Cosmic Intelligence. It starts with the great principle of Cause, from which proceeds Effects. Everything takes place within the 'Universal,' or Divine Intelligence, and not outside it. When we merge our mind with the consciousness of our inner being in relationship to the Cause Consciousness of our Creator, we will progress very rapidly, by experiencing the Active Principles of Creative Thought Force.

The intrinsic value of these Laws is that we must begin by searching within ourselves for the basic truths. We must come to be aware of our make-up, operation and control of every part. Before we can become the expressor of the fullness of Life, our basic nature of thinking and emotional reactions, of apparent conflict between our inner and outer self, must be understood.

The Cosmic Plan of Life is that we eventually come to realize that we are not individual persons, but rather, are important parts that fit into a *complete being* expressing itself in the highest degree of its knowledge with Cosmic Feeling. We are in this stage of growth by choice, to return to the Original Position for which we were created, to be one with Cosmic Consciousness, as Co-Creators.

Everyone is born with a destiny and is given repeated opportunities to fulfull it. There is no actual time involved, as we know it, but there is an end to opportunities. Every case is different; therefore, this will vary according to each individual. All have many lessons to be learned, that they may progress toward greater oneness of expression with the Infinite Being.

The Cosmic Laws operate for the advancement of all souls to higher levels, or states of being. They do not permit enforcement of one will upon another, to the point of degradation. They do not permit any being to dictate, use force, or threaten those to whom free will is granted. In so imposing will upon them, they then would not be responsible for their actions. Our free will gives us the right to choose our destiny, and to be responsible for that which we set into motion.

The Basic Law of the Universe grants each and every individual independence and freedom of choice, so that each may learn from his experiences. It is the privilege of everyone to direct his own Life and shape his own destiny, even though it be by the path of trial and error. No one has the right to interfere in the affairs or free will choice of others. The Law applies equally to all. One may counsel or instruct, but never interfere.

The Law allows us to be responsible for our Life and to be supportive of others, as they progress to achieve the same thing. It allows every individual to be all he is, by giving all free choice. As we progress, one step at a time, in our understanding of the Cosmic Laws, we eventually become aware that our purpose in Life is to grow. The more we are elevated by our application of the Law, the more we are gifted with the ability to assist our fellow beings to grow also.

Anything contrary to the Cosmic Principles must be corrected before one can be in order with it. One cannot separate his self from the Cause Consciousness; therefore, unjust acts result in a constant demand by our inner consciousness for corrections to be made. The longer these corrections are avoided by a stubborn or proud mind, the greater the penalty that must be paid in time. This comes in various ways, for no one can escape his responsibilities.

We are required to warn those that we believe to be ignorant of a chosen course of action which violates an important Natural Law, with the resulting consequences being a detriment to them. After being warned, our duty ends. If the person insists on continuing as before, it becomes his sole responsibility. We must recognize the right of every individual to exercise complete free will, which includes the right to be wrong, so long as it does not infringe upon the rights of others.

When the act threatens others, including other planets or planes of existence, only then may the individual or group responsible be forcibly restrained. Force or restraint may be used onlt when the rights of others are very seriously endangered. Restraints, whether by force or unseen, are of only temporary use. Education, which will raise the ethical level of a person or group, is the only permanent solution.

The manner of administering education requires exercising great care, through gradual preparation, to alter the pattern of Life to a more stable atmosphere conducive to learning, and applying the knowledge and understanding gained. This gradual awareness and grasping of concepts of a higher truth come with evolvement of the soul, mind and body. These are ever striving upward toward perfection and oneness with the Source. Thus Life is an endless variety of continual growth. The process of evolution operates according to the free choice of each and every person, in every phase of existence.

All planets and their inhabitants must pass through the orderly stages of evolvement, from lower to higher, with few exceptions. Each world must 'obtain' its own destiny. Any assistance by another planet must be definitely and greatly limited by Universal Law, in order to maintain a timed pattern of evolution.

When an outside agency threatens to endanger a planet or people, only then may direct interference come from other planets to counterbalance this condition, so that the planned development may continue. And, when an endless repetition of growth and destruction affects the orderly or natural process of a planet's natives, then those from other planets may indirectly influence, or educate within the limits of the Universal Law. A higher civilization can actually destroy a lesser one without intent, by imposing its wisdom on those who cannot understand or absorb it.

According to the Cosmic Plan of the Universal Laws, the people of other planets cannot directly affect the destiny of our planet, country, or people. They can only give us assistance within the limits of the Laws. It is the duty of each person on our world to act for himself and work for peace.

H13   "We are presently being threatened by the potential of engaging ourselves in a nuclear war which would inevitably mean the end of our human race. These conditions can only be altered by other worlds when: (1) we, the inhabitants of Earth, express consent for intervention in our affairs, or (2) we directly violate the Universal Laws. Otherwise, a limited atomic war could not be contained.

After the planet Maldek was destroyed by several hydrogen bombs, which reduced it to

an asteroid belt, a new policy was legislated
in the Galactic Pax regulations. This law now
states that:

"We, of the Galactic Confederation of
Planets, can only intervene in a planet's
affairs and evolution when the following conditions exist:

"1. When a planet—either a member or non-
member of the Confederation constitutes a
threat to the existence of its neighbors.

"Any nuclear exchange on Earth would have
immediate disastrous effects on other inhabited planets in our system. Your planet cannot be allowed to blast itself into dust, as
it forms a vital part of the solar system and
would destroy the gravitational equilibrium
of the whole. Further, it would cut off light
from the outer planets were it to become an
asteroid belt.

"2. When a planet is threatened by an outside cosmic influence from which it cannot
avoid harmful effects in an encounter.

"Your transit through a concentration of
cosmic particles in space, plus your own nuclear experiments, has been spewing forth
radioactive particles or waste into the atmosphere, harmful to all inhabitants of Earth.
As a result of these outside influences which
are upsetting the planet's axis, there are going to be severe geological changes. The
Earth may reverse its north and south poles.

"3. When the Galactic Tribunal is so
ordered to act by the Guardians (or counselors)
existing in the higher realms.

"Because of your diversified attributes and

potentials, along with being a part of the overall evolutionary pattern of this galactic system, you will most definitely be preserved or
saved from extinction."

All people throughout the Universe are related to one another, because the same Great
Creator made us all. War or any form of conflict between neighbors should be outlawed
formally as the means to an end. It is contrary not only to the laws of man, but to the
Laws of the Universe, the Laws of Intelligence,
and to the Laws of the Maker of Laws.

A   "It is a Cosmic Axiom that, "Each one moves
inexorably toward the state of Absolute Perfection." The Cosmic Plan is for a united people on each planet, with minds aware of the
vast concept of Life, and its continuance. We
need to understand the Universal Laws involved
in our thoughts and actions. Only a deep inner
feeling of brotherhood with all people will
bring about the awareness which produces Love
and Harmony. We can never hope to be awakened
to the Universal Truth if we are continually
stormed on all sides by talk of war, bombs,
murder and strife. We cannot ignore the fact
that every time we so much as speak in anger
to another, we are flouting the Laws of the
Maker of Laws."

The Cosmos is a Creation built by our God
through Love and Intelligence (Light), resulting in an orderly Creation. The Guardians, or
Elder Brothers, are administrators of the Universal Law, and oversee all human affairs. The
same Laws apply to every being as they do
to the Cosmos. These Cosmic Principles are
working in and through all living beings.
This fact makes all Life One. In each and
every part of the Universe, all things abide
and function according to the Law. To under-

stand these Laws of Reality will enable us to use them for our own good in every aspect of Life.

As we intently study the workings and manifestations of the Creator, the results of our quest make it possible to fathom the Divine Plan, within limits, and to order our lives accordingly. We find that each new discovery and application of the Laws of the Universe brings us into closer contact with the Creative Spirit. "Law is the confinement of Creation in an acting principle of ordained authority. It manifests as a governing force. It is the Presence of the Infinite Being in the Law it has sent forth to maintain its own Creation." The ways of God are immutable and apparent only to those who have spiritual discernment.

We must *think for ourselves* in order to gain a practical knowledge of the Laws of the Creator. When we surrender this basic right, we permit others to restrain our free choice by selecting what they think is right for us to know and accept. Each of us must do his own work of rebuilding. We must merge our thinking with the Whole Creation instead of confining our thoughts to ourselves or permitting others to censor them. The Universal Laws are the basic principles upon which perfect Harmony of full accord in thoughts and actions are achieved. They respect the rights of all Creation within the Father, Mother, God, in which all live, move, and have their being.

Separation between ourselves and the Giver of all Life only occurs when we exalt ourselves above the Creator, through ignorance. Those who work in opposition to Cosmic Law usually trap themselves, by violation of the rights of others. The only hell there is, is self created, by living contrary to the Laws of Universal Life. Everyone creates and is responsible for, his reality. Our lives are a reflection of our knowledge, experience, and understanding of these Laws as they affect the Three Primary Phases of our complete awareness.

The Laws of the Universe and the Forces of Nature, or "Natural Laws" were designed by the Creator for the good of all Life, and made unchangeable. Universal Law is provided for the harmonious existence of all beings on all levels of evolutionary progression. The Eternal laws are simple.

We, in error, can create complications with the natural flow of Life all around us. When the Natural Laws are followed, the results of their application is simple. But when one is made to conflict with another, the results are usually complicated. Seek the simple way to accomplish that which you desire. Keep complexity to a minimum. The greatest concepts of the Universe are harnessed and employed by means so simple it would astound us.

We are now turning on our fellow beings the Forces of Nature which would otherwise be our servants, if we would use them as intended, for *benefit* instead of destruction. By misusing the Universal Forces, we become slaves and forfeit our mastery of them. When this occurs, we are in deep trouble. Only a radical change in *philosophy* can reinstate the Right and the Good, and make us once more the masters of our destinies.

We have been taught contrary to the principles of the Cosmos through the ages; therefore, we naturally distrust new ideas or thoughts when they do not blend with our previous knowledge. Sometimes the concepts are

somewhat difficult to explain to minds already
set. These higher Laws should be regarded as
part of the everyday facts of Life. However,
the environment in which we live forces us to
comply with certain social and ethical perfor-
mances. The Laws of man are often good, but
at best, they are only misinterpretations of
the Universal Laws.

As a rule, we set standards for our individual Life, and a standard is the degree or
quality of influence or guidance. These Basic
Laws or rules could be called 'Principles in
Action,' which quickly regulate these standards
and rules. In truth, regulation means the unifying or the drawing of all into one, which is
the real meaning of Law. Everyone has his own
standard. We have a set of laws to which we
adhere. We have the general laws of our planet,
but there is something more than judicial laws.

The Universal Laws were given to guide us
in correcting our ways, when things have di-
gressed beyond the Will of our Almighty Father.
These basic truths can only inform us how to
overcome our difficulties. It is our free will
choice to accept them and change ourselves. If
we refuse, we attract or bring about troubles
upon ourselves, and we can blame no one else
for the consequences. The level of our comprehension of them determines our capacity to fulfill and apply the Creative Laws of the Universe and how we can grow as a result of abid-
ing by them.

When we cooperate with the Laws of Creation
our Divine Rights are assured; but when we break
them, we suffer the results. We should adhere
to them not solely as a matter of ethics, but
because we know that the results of defying them
will be very unpleasant for us. One thereby

learns that living according to the Laws of Our Radiant One *elevates* us, through an upward spiral of progress along the pathway of eternal Life. By Universal Law all things tend upwards to a state of absolute perfection.

Actually, there is only the Great *Law of One*, Cause and Effect, with twelve basic aspects. These Natural Laws serve to unify the development of the Spiritual, Social and Material Phases, or basic areas of our Life. All operates by Infinite Laws. Trial and Error are only necessary when we lack understanding of the complete principles by which everything is maintained. Only when we learn through our own mistakes will we be prepared to return to unity with All Life, and oneness with its Source.

The Cosmic Laws are only effective in resolving common problems when we condition ourselves to overcome living by half-truths, and imperfect impressions. These cause our actions to be out of balance, as well as the effects that follow. Here are the basic principles of our Life. Therefore, they bring into our experience certain things, because of our misuse of them. Practicing these Laws is the important thing. All the Force in the Conscious Universe is set into motion by us, as soon as our Thought becomes the Word. We are the Co-Creator, Master and Expressor of the fullness of Life, through free will choice.

We must know ourselves and become conscious of our total being and potential as the creator and regulator of this power that channels through us and our thought processes. One of two things can occur: We can feel our independence, doing little about it, or we can recognize our potential as the Father-Mother-God in operation. Therefore, *know* that we are literally the manifestation or offspring of the

Trinity of Power, known as the Primary Laws of
Life, Light, and Love, of the One God.

The Natural Laws are ours to direct, and if
we do not direct their Forces with our intelligence, then they command us, because we are
a part of them. Our desire activates one or
more of the Laws at any given moment, and we
draw upon their Powers, which act through us
to the degree we permit and control them. However, there are restrictions to the misuse of
them. When we realize that we have this capability to guide the Trinity of Force, we will
have a Cause Consciousness of All Reality.
Consciousness is a certain knowing of that
which is Real.

All of our problems come from a shortsight-
edness in ignoring the Universal Will or Laws
of Life, as found in All Nature. Regardless
of the stage of evolution, *the cause of all
discord is the shutting off of Divine Expression.* It is our divine purpose to simply recognize the Cosmic Will as forces or principles
to perpetuate Life, and to permit them to manifest freely through our experiences. This is
our only solution in comprehending and correcting the Basic Cause of our problems on our
planet Earth, as we build a united world and
New Age.

When we act in ignorance and oppose the Creative Will with our own personal will, we simply direct our small portion of the Life Force,
and oppose it to the Original Central Will
Force of the Universe. This results in our
being overcome by the effect of such an action
of opposition.

However, when we use our inner divinity, we
need no personal will, for we can then 'Tune

In and Channel' the unlimited Will Energy of
the All Spirit in a wise manner. When we recognize our oneness with Cosmic Cause and begin
to use its Laws, we will have no further need
of a teacher, for Law gave us Life, and it will
be our instructor.

Our Inner Self already knows these higher
Laws, which chart the Pathway of Progress for
us. Every sane being, deep within, knows that
which is right and that which is wrong. It is
not so much that we do not know, but that we
may not yet accept the fact that it is a matter of *survival* to act according to what we
know. It is essential that we learn and follow these higher Laws. In the Cosmic Age in
which we are living, we will and must learn the
definite use of our God potential, of the Law
of Life in our own being, for our survival.
We will depend on the use of these Laws in the
future, for our survival.

There is no half way, for we must go all the
way in observing and fulfilling the Laws of
Truth, the Basic Laws of Life. One cannot
close his eyes to these Basic Laws of the Universe. The primary cause of evil in the world
is ignorance of the Universal Laws. This is
the reason for all our imbalances, and all
forms of Life are being affected, especially
the human race. The material bonds which each
individual has allowed to govern his thinking
will demand the right of existence. As a result, there is conflict between Natural Law
and unnatural law, or the truth of the future
and the habits of the past.

The Unnamable is the sole First Cause in
the Universe, becoming, by philosophical exten-
sion, the Creator of all things, even though
it employed other means to accomplish the actual Creation. A group of equals, called the

Eloh-im, or Elder Race, were first created to perform the task of the Creation, including lesser man. The Universal Laws were created as acting principles, to maintain the continuance of the process of creation, development, and transmutation of the Creative Spirit within the Cosmic Consciousness, or the All.

Each of us is an integral part of the Cosmic Consciousness, as the Life of the form. It is proper to call this the Father, for it is the parent of all form Life. This is the foundation of the concept of Life, for we can see conscious Life manifesting through all forms. Many people are now beginning to realize the importance of consciousness, rather than the mind. Eventually some will begin to live the principles of the Cosmos, as taught throughout the Universe, as there are many beneficial results obtained through the application of the Laws of Life.

We are truly students of Universal cause, as we observe the Natural Laws manifesting themselves in many forms of expression in every form of Life. These basic concepts can be applied by anyone who will take the time to consider and think about them. It is an unending search for knowledge, for we, as finite creatures, can never hope to fully understand the Infinite. Although it only requires a lifetime of study and living to gain its underlying Wisdom.

We must consider applying an effort to the understanding of the Universal Laws of our being while we are yet in the physical body. When we leave it for another dimension without having expressed that of which we were capable while in the body, it will then be very difficult for us to experience mastery.

We can know how to live entirely within the Laws of the Radiant One, if we would only open our minds to a *vision of the whole,* and consider them as a natural part of Life. Such self discipline, on a constant basis, would give each of us the necessary control so that our Inner Being would be absolute master, rather than to permit the body, emotions, or the mind to be in control. As a result, change could swiftly envelop the planet. Then there could be a true sense of equality, for all of us are meant to live the fundamentals of the Universal Laws rightly applied under the guiding hand of the Most High.

★   ★   ★

THE UNIVERSAL LAWS

0.
CENTRAL FORCE

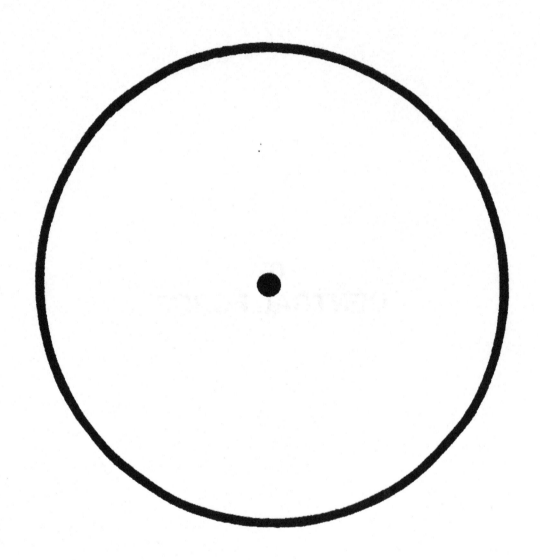

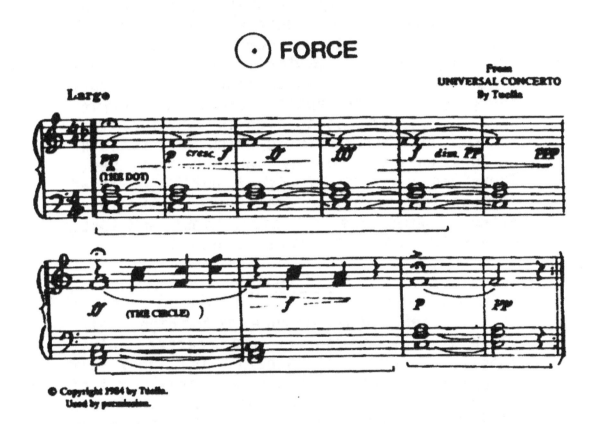

Number	Symbol	Law	Color	Tone
0.	⊙	Central Force	White	A

"The Source Thought Force is the Cause and Creator of All Things."

PRINCIPLE

2   "At the Center of the Universe is the generation point of all energy. As we are Conscious in the center of our being, so we are. From this Source of Central Force all the Laws of the Universe become manifest." The Primary Energy Flow of the Central Force, which permeates all space, is so high in Vibration that it has no characteristic which will register on our physical senses or any instrument. Therefore, it is *unmanifest* until converted through some means, and manifests as the three primary principles of Life, Light and Love. We are an 'Image' of Creative Spirit.

THREE PHASES

1. *Spirit,* or mental core, is the high self, which directly comes from the Creative Spirit Itself, of which it is part. Our inner self exists indefinitely. Each is a small part of the Greater Whole. The spirit part of each self is directly from the Source, and is an integral part of Its Immortal and Eternal Being.

2. *Soul* is the middle self, which carries all inherited memory patterns and instincts. It assumes responsibility for all of the details of repeated embodiments. This process involves a temporary period of memory absence, requires that these patterns of thought must be consciously expressed through the medium of the physical brain cells for a considerable length

of time to *fully open*, develop, or change awareness, as desired.

3. *Material form* is the low self. The human body is the covering of the spirit; its presence is necessary to function on our physical plane of existence. This outer form is perishable and transitory. It is the least important part of our being, and is an elementary physiochemical animal form. It is made of atoms from the One Common Source.

To the best of our knowledge, the Universe is composed of Cosmic Intelligence, Force, and Form. We know that out of this Creative Intelligence emerges all manifestation. Force can be measured as an impulse, and Form as an object. But the Creator of both, the Father-Mother principle, is often beyond our comprehension. Therefore, the Infinite Creator is sometimes called, 'The Unnamable,' because it is believed that no word can create the correct mental picture of Deity. A mind contained within a mortal and finite body cannot, by its very nature, correctly comprehend that which is Immortal and Infinite, because it has no standards of comparison.

There are two ways of recognizing God. One is, that the Omnipotent, Creative Force is the One Great Reality; and the second is, that God is a vital, dynamic, conscious personality within us. Both have their purpose: one is to teach and reveal to us our Oneness with all Life, and that we are a co-creator in this Universe. The second is to give us a direct, vital, and personal contact with God. Life is the divine energy of the Infinite One which is operating within us.

K2   "The Solar Logos, the divine All In All, the Trinity, is expressed on all levels in all of the Creator's manifestations, as the Father positive, Mother negative, and Issue, a product of the two forces. The inner spirit of every living being is the negative spiritual body, within the physical, and with this combination Life is made manifest. Every cell of the positive material body contains within it a nucleus of the negative spirit. A point ● is a term for negative spirit within a circle ◯ of material substance forming a dot within a circle ⊙. The dot is the immortal soul, and the outer circle is the positive material vehicle for it."

When we control this Central Force of our being to the extent that it can be directed *at will* to any other being, we develop a oneness with all Life. We inherit a Great Creative Force, which will assist us in our growth through cooperative efforts, even in the face of adverse conditions. Once this Force is applied for constructive purposes, it will change our Life toward the better road of progress. When we learn to allow this Force to envelop and flow through our being, we will then fulfill our primary purpose—to manifest the Power of the Creator—through the Trinity of Life, Light, and Love, on the physical level of being.

*   *   *

1.
LIFE

LIFE

Number	Symbol	Law	Color	Tone
1.	⊕	Life	Blue	G

"Life is the carrier of progression in its eternal and infinite spiral."

PRINCIPLE

Life is growth. All things throughout the Cosmos are in a state of evolution. Evolution operates according to the free choice of each and every individual. Life is *perpetual motion,* for Creation is ever constant. Re-creation is a privilege only given to those who are evolving to a point where they are in the Image of the Immortal Godhead. When one falls low enough in this pattern of growth, he no longer has the ability to re-create. As a result, everything then becomes opposite to the Creation, and they actually cause destruction instead of re-creation. *Life is the great positive. It is the Father of all Creation.*

THREE PHASES

1. It is our spiritual purpose to attain reunion with our immortal consciousness, made in the Image and likeness of God. Spiritual growth is the universal desire for freedom, liberty and worship of One Creator, along with equality for all.

2. In order to gain true Life, we must lose the aspect of self, which is only for self, and become aware of our personal identity in service to all Life, in oneness with the creative purpose of growth for everyone. We are all one and an integral part of God.

B12   3. "The Life Force enters into our whole being by the Four Essential Functions of:

a. Thought; b. Motion;   c. Breathing;   and
d. Food. Health consists of the equally balanced
development of these vital expressions. Health
is the normal and natural condition of Life."

Life manifests itself only when there is a
precise interchange of relative power of Primary Force in motion through imbalanced opposites. When positive and negative lines of
force or bands cross, both poles of equal density and vibration form a vortex. The whirlpool then condenses into a particular creation
of Life. By phasing this interchange, unlimited power through motion or vibration is the
result. When the power exceeds the differential phase, disintegration will result.

The Universe is kept in perpetual motion
because of its imbalance seeking an equilibrium. Were it ever to achieve a balance, all
motion would cease. Every celestial body that
rotates on a magnetic axis represents a balance of motion in the form of imbalance, which
is constantly seeking an equilibrium. Motion
can exist only when there is an imbalance be-
between two or more poles of force. That which
is in balance cannot move of itself, without
some other force causing the action.

The galactic, solar, molecular, and atomic
systems are powered and controlled by tapping
into the Primary Force, with their activated
components converting it into Four Secondary
Forces or effects in motion.

10   "The outer circle is eternal Source all,
that you call *God*, for it unfolds in the arms
of Love, that meet. It has no beginning and
no ending, and so it is eternity. The central
core is the microcosm of the expression of the
macrocosm. The flow of Life from the Source
enters the microcosm in four manifestations

through the Four Forces. All that IS can be related through the outer circle, inner core, four quadrants, flow around, within, and back to the circle, in the movement of Life energy which is eternal."

15   "Life is a perpetual motion of regeneration. To generate is to set into motion. Regeneration is the constant continuance of the generating motion, which continually reactivates and propels itself. The Creator being eternal, expresses the Life Force through perpetual motion. There is no death, only the transference of Life, or Spirit pattern of energy."

Spirit Energy is the cause or active principle of all changes which occur in the Universe, and through which it has a demonstrable reality of existence. In all states of consciousness there is motion. Without motion there is nothing. We can only know motion through the relationship between one phase of expression and another. All Life is powered by the same energy of perpetual motion. Creation is the result of polarized energy and matter throughout infinite space, with both following a pattern of constant formation, development, and transmutation.

* * *

2.
MAGNETIC RESONANCE

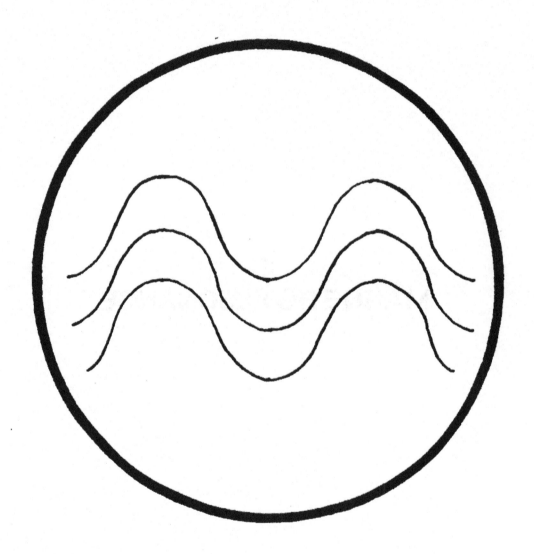

⊜ RESONATING MAGNETISM

From
UNIVERSAL CONCERTO
By Toella

Number	Symbol	Law	Color	Tone
2.	⊜	Magnetic Resonance	Blue-Green	G♭

"The Magnetic lines of thought force bind and connect everything together through alternating Resonance, with the Source."

PRINCIPLE

Magnetic energy is a level of vibrations that is concerned with establishing polarity, or balancing current flowing between two points or poles as force. Resonance is the frequency at which an animate or inanimate form will absorb energy waves. This depends upon the composition, shape, and dimensions. Magnetic Resonance is the force which holds planets, suns, and even entire galaxies in their orbits. Without its causing the continual action of Re-creation, nothing whatsoever would exist.

THREE PHASES

1. God creates by superimposing an oscillating charge of thought force upon the infinite point of space. That is, a vortex is established which constantly exerts its influence on the unmanifest, thus creating energy, and in consequence, matter.

2. We are linked with one another by Magnetic Resonance, as our energy fields of Life interact as one body within the Universe.

3. A field of Resonating force gives Magnetism the property which makes it distinct and unique. There are three phases, or types of polarity charges that create the complete trinity of power principle.

K2   "Any recognition of things unseen falls into
a spiritual realm, and of things seen, into a
material realm. There is much very real Magnetic Resonance energy in everything, or neither
could exist. Both exist, so both contain this
same common energy, which maintains the entire
Universe and puts it all into Creation. Magnetic Resonance is the freest energy there is,
and the most powerful. This Universal Energy
encompasses all."

     "Magnetic Resonance is the breath of Life
Force that is breathed into every living thing,
both animate and inanimate. This is the gift
of the Creator, the very channel of all His expression. Without this energy of Magnetic Resonance there would be no existence, no variety,
no reproduction. All that is created stands
as proof of its existence."

     "The real being, the Magnetic one is that
which puts us into operation. The real being
is the spiritual body, the astral body, or the
molecular energy body that dwells within the
form of flesh. This body, unseen by physical
eyes, is the everlasting, immortal body that
knows no death, therefore, is more real than
the physical form or shell that is quickly created and later falls into dust. We are the
magnificent Image that lives eternally."

A   "The Magnetic field of influence which sur-
rounds every form and pervades all space is
like the series of circular *ripples* created by
dropping a pebble into a pond. These wave
fronts move outward from the center point, expanding in size, but diminishing in force similar to 'Direct Current' as they move. However, when two pebbles are simultaneously
dropped into the pond several feet apart, two
sets of expanding circular waves are created,
moving outward from each central point. Where

the wave fronts meet, an elliptical interference pattern is formed, with its smaller ends extending between the two central points. Although both wave fronts diminish in force as they travel outward from their central points, the ellipse pattern combines a portion of both forces to create a third force of *Resonance* similar to 'Alternating Current,' which remains constant between the two central points so long as they remain active.

These circular waves or ripples create Magnetic lines of force between bodies of space, which constantly alternate their direction of flow by a two-way pulse of Resonance. Such alternating elliptical fields of force, extending between every body, are the unseen bonds which balance the Universe."

The recognition of this tremendous energy factor of Magnetic Resonance will bring us to fully realize our immortal spiritual body and nature of it. In using this energy we will become fully aware of our true place in Creation, in relation to our Creator. In this complete awakening and wise use of Magnetic Resonance energy, we will create a New Age, in every respect.

*   *   *

3.
ACTION AND REACTION

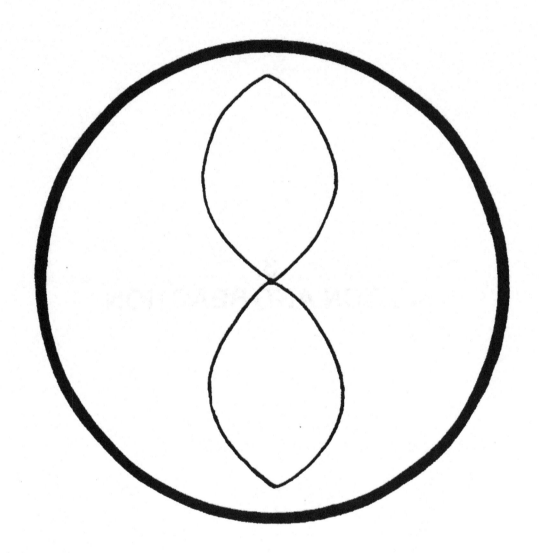

⊗ ACTION AND REACTION

From
UNIVERSAL CONCERTO
By Tuella

Number	Symbol	Law	Color	Tone
3.	Ⓧ	Action & Reaction	Green	F

"For every Action, there is an equal and opposite Reaction."

PRINCIPLE

Once we have set a series of actions in motion, they must continue to their final conclusion, which will occur sooner or later, but it is certain. We cannot change that which is our past, but we can alter the course of our future in any manner chosen. We have free will, and are subject to the changing pattern of our thoughts, emotions and consequent future actions. It is never too late to change the pattern of one's Life.

THREE PHASES

1. Creative thought in Action is the Primary Cause. Out of this center of Cause, resulting Reactions, or effects, will follow.

2. That which we convey in our thoughts, feelings, and Actions, is most often what we will receive in Reactions. Most of us have not yet learned complete control of our expressions.

3. All Actions take place in time by the interchange of the forces of Nature. Everything has some effect on everything else in the Universe. "Creation is the consequence of Cause and Effect."

Action and Reaction, or *compensation*, is worked out to the infinite degree in vibratory rate, so when we create an error of negation, the balance is upset and a negative Reaction occurs. The error of negation is created only by our ignorance of equality. Cause and Effect exacts an equal degree through interaction. The principle of Action and Reaction requires nothing of us except a perfect balance in all phases of Life.

It is one thing to be intelligent, by acquiring knowledge; it is another to use intelligence by acquiring wisdom to control its Actions and Reactions. To acquire wisdom, we must progress in our understanding of the psychological motives behind our innumerable thoughts of everyday Life. Before we can become the expressors of the fullness of Life, our basic natures of thinking and emotional Reactions, of apparent conflict between our inner and outer selves, must be understood.

Each one of us creates and becomes responsible for our reality. Our Lives are a reflection of our knowledge, experience, and understanding of the Law of Action and Reaction. It is our privilege to act and react as we choose. All the Force in the Conscious Universe is set into motion by us, as soon as our thoughts become words. We are the Co-Creator, Master and Expressor of the fullness of Life, through free will choice.

B12   "When we act in ignorance and oppose the Creative Will of Central Force, we simply direct our small portion of the Force of Life, and oppose it to that of the entire Universe. As a consequence, our being is overcome by the effect of such an action of opposition. This is the reason for all our imbalances, and all forms of Life are affected, especially us. We can see from the ruins of other civilizations on Earth that Reaction is the cataclysmic balance for wrong Action."

Anything contrary to Nature must be corrected before we can be in Harmony with it. We cannot separate ourselves from the Cause Consciousness; therefore, unjust Actions result in a constant Reaction of demand by our inner consciousness to correct such conditions. The longer these corrections are avoided by us, the greater the inevitable repercussions we will experience.

When the results of our thoughts and Actions are good, then the path we are following guides us toward constructive purposes for the benefit of the whole. When the results of our thoughts and Actions are evil, then the path we are following guides us toward destructive purposes for the benefit of self alone. Through our choice we thereby set in motion the cause of every effect which influences our Lives and others'.

A   "Through studying deeply the Actions and Reactions of Nature, many satisfactory results can be obtained. Natural conditions set up a variety of effects, many of which can be anticipated, others of which cannot. Nature herself has a tendency to perform in unexpected ways, especially when interfered with by our efforts."

*   *   *

4.
VIBRATION

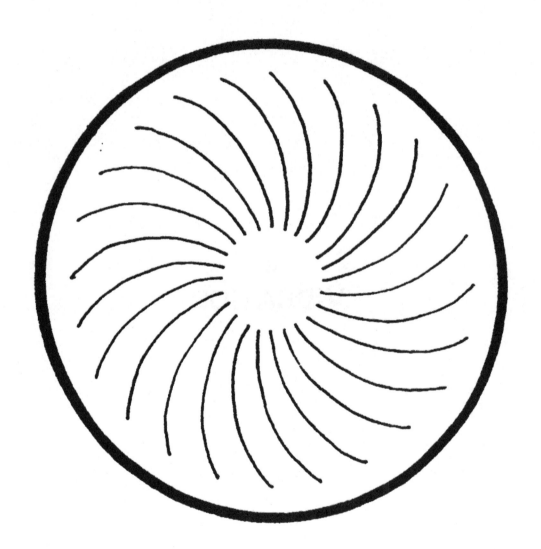

VIBRATION

Number	Symbol	Law	Color	Tone
4.	✸	Vibration	Green-Yellow	F^b

"Everything in the entire Universe moves by Vibration, or frequencies."

PRINCIPLE

Being is Vibration. Vibration is alive, dynamic and very, very active in the Universe. Everything vibrates, from the smallest atom up to the largest galactic universe in space--all is in motion. Everything in Creation has its own identifying Vibration. The frequency under which a form functions can be established only by itself. The higher frequency manifests a faster period of development, while the lower promotes a slower period of growth.

THREE PHASES

1. Our personal Vibration is the only important part of our being, because it is our relationship to the Original Thought of our Creation.

2. Vibration is created by thought, and through it, we qualify this ever-flowing energy with whatever we desire it to manifest in our Life and world.

3. The human brain and body are emitters of the entire spectrum of waves or rays. Each part and organ has its distinct frequency. The movement of forces is vibratory.

Spirit is energy. Each individual manifestation and unit composing it, in every form, in the macrocosm or microcosm, is energy, each vibrating and responding to its own personal vibration, at a particular rate. Everything exists within a certain frequency limit or bandwidth of energy. No two vibrations in Creation are exactly alike.

B12   "The spectrum is made up of Vibrations that come in 'Octaves of Power' (variations of eight) in the whole scheme of things. The rate of Vibration varies. For basic health, the most important octaves are:

Octave	Phase	Modulator
58	Thought Waves	Color
50	Life, or Food Enzymes	Sound
48	Cells of human body	Sound

"We are the selector of the octave that we desire to affect us. Free will is the vibra- tion that modulates us. Vibrations should al- ways lift us, and not be allowed to pull us downward, or to reduce our vital power. We can modulate our Life into whatever we want it to be. Take away the Vibrations which modu- late us downward, and add those which modulate us upward. Its power is achieved as simply as that."

"To modulate or change our individual vibra- tions—or spiritual, mental, and physical from low, to medium, to high—we must realize that every other vibration outside of us tends to modulate us either upward (positive charge), midway (neutral or stationary charge), or down- ward (negative charge) continually. The range or spectrum of Vibrations in the Universe is considerable."

"For example, in the range of Thought Waves or octave 58, simplistic thoughts cause us to modulate upward (positive charge), and complex thoughts cause us to modulate downward (nega- tive charge). This pertains equally to both

our own thoughts and those of others that influence us. Mental or subliminal capsulations
can modulate us by Vibration, color, and sound
projections."

"The same principle in the range of Life, or
Food Enzymes or octave 50, living foods, causes
us to modulate upward (positive charge), and
dead foods cause us to modulate downward (negative charge). Food is the needed chemical
elements which the human body requires in order to conduct the vital Life energy throughout effectively."

We can raise or lower the Vibration of the
atoms composing our bodies through the energy
created by thought. The frequency or speed
at which the electrons and protons travel in
their orbits around the nucleus is caused by
the manifestation of the Universal Pulse.
These atomic pulses or Vibrations of the Cosmic Root Force flow through certain energy centers of the body into the central seed atom in
the brain which functions as the focal point
for their development and consolidation of one
composite Vibration. This atom in turn uni-
formly distributes the polarized pulse of Life
to the magnetic field of force, or aura, surrounding the body.

*   *   *

5.
LIGHT

 **LIGHT**

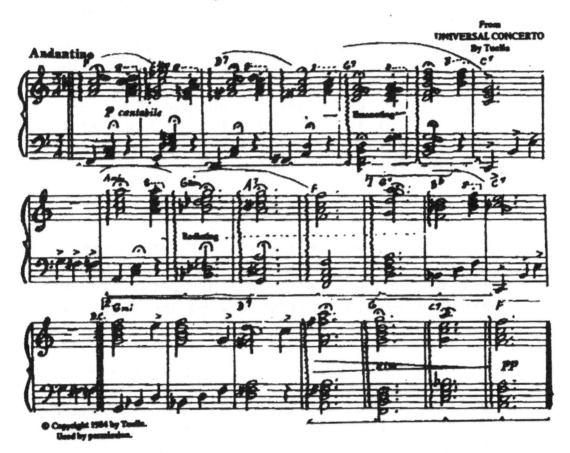

Number	Symbol	Law	Color	Tone
5.	⬤	Light	Yellow	E

"Light is the One Pure, Primal Essence out of which comes all Creation."

PRINCIPLE

Everywhere about us is a Universal Substance called 'Cosmic Light' and which many refer to as Spirit. It is the pure Life Substance of the first Cause, God. Light is substance, energy, and luminosity, all three in one. This is Infinite, and we may draw upon It at any time for whatever we require. This Pure Light Force is the Limitless Storehouse of the Universe. In It is All Perfection, and out of It comes All that IS. *Light is the great neutral. It is the Mother of All Creation.*

THREE PHASES

1. A central Light dwells at the center of our being. This Light is the star of Divine Will of the Cosmos. From the center all the Rays of Creation proceed, out of the One. All Rays are carriers of Forces.

2. Light is the Power of Higher Intelligence to tune in and control Will. We may use it to guide and conduct the Life Energy to accomplish things of a constructive nature. To attempt misuse of the Light to harm others would result immediately in self destruction instead.

3. All that we are able to experience in a physical Universe is composed of Light, or the basic building block of our Creator. Light is the unchangeable Essence of all things.

K2   "Seek within, for the One Light of the God

Spark which exists within all beings created
of the One Creator, or Truth. Everyone IS a
Divine Spark of the Creator, and this Spark IS
deep within us or we would not exist. Seek
this in sincerity of motive, in responsibility
of thought, in balance of being, and we will
find the Truth which lies eternal within the
Core of all things. When we allow Light (Truth)
to pervade our consciousness, it strikes this
Spark within and grows into an ever brighter
Light, which influences others."

3   "Light is the combined manifestations of
Intelligence and Force which extend from out
of the Primary Source. It represents the Omnipresent and Omnipotent One. The functions of
the Light are inherent in Itself, and will always operate in the correct manner. The Light
is invoked to nullify any influence that
threatens to disrupt your balanced field of
force, or aura. To Invoke the Light is to
bring Divine Intelligence and Power into the
activity of the moment. In the beginning there
was the Word, or the Light or our Radiant One,
the most encompassing emanation in All That IS.
Therefore, it is one of the three primary principles active in Creation, that exist for the
purpose of its continuance."

The goal of the moment which is eternal, in
a sense, must always be kept before us, ever
shining like a great golden sun, with eyes that
see its Light. To stay within its brilliance,
permitting it to envelop our being in its
Power, and guide our destiny as the Creative
Spirit feels is best for us. When we use our
inherent inner Light, we need no personal will,
for we can then *tune into* the Will of the Radiant One and utilize this unlimited Power in
a wise manner. By putting spiritual intuition
before human power, our desire becomes purpose,
and the result is always of benefit for all.

Light is constructive and beneficial once applied. The Light simply needs to be called upon. Prayer is a power; it can heal and stop conflict when done correctly, or in unison.

Every thought, emotion, and action is reflected and recorded in the Light of our own individual aura. We may imagine a thought as a Spark of Light, with rays extending equally in all directions, as a sphere at any point of its expansion. Light, once manifested as Creative Thought, will extend indefinitely unless intercepted by some one or object capable of absorbing and dissipating that particular emanation of energy.

In the Light all things appear as they are in reality. All is eternal Light throughout space, the reverse of darkness which is only an illusion created by the false thoughts of material consciousness. All who come out of the illusion of darkness into the Light will never again lose themselves in the illusion. Too great a preponderance of darkness or evil invariably results in self destruction and a new beginning in heavier densities of matter. The choice is up to each individual, for every mortal being has been equally endowed with free will.

*   *   *

6.
MIND

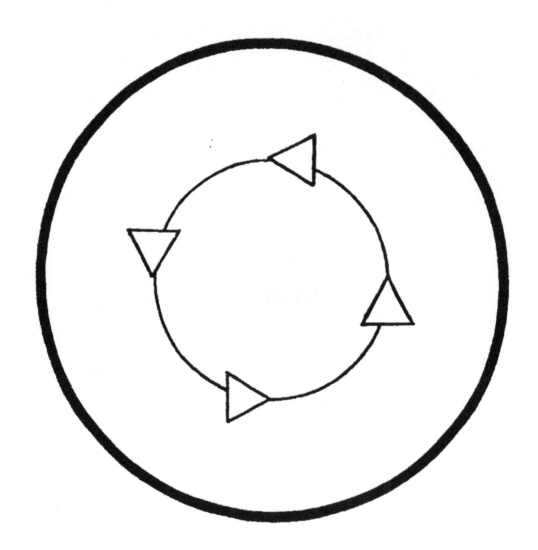

MIND

Number	Symbol	Law	Color	Tone
6.	⊕	Mind	Orange-yellow	E^b

"The Mind is an energy form, which is part of what goes into Creation."

PRINCIPLE

F   "All Minds are as One, and the energies form-ing matter are a part of it likewise. The All-Mind is known as the Almighty, Creator, and God. It controls the Universe to the limits possible. While each person is part of the All-Mind, the Conscious individuality is not controlled by It to the extent of interference in the affairs of the Consciousness. It can suggest, guide, or direct, but it cannot control. The indi-vidual Conscious thought force is the primary activity, or direction of growth."

THREE PHASES

1.   All is Universal Mind. God is Mind and Spirit. All that exists is in the All-Mind. Mind is neutral. It cannot emanate energy, but only direct the flow and action of energy. Universal Mind permeates all things.

2.   All use the Intelligence of the All-Mind, with no individual having a mind of his own. Each only uses that portion of the Infinite Mind that he is capable of absorbing.

3.   The brain is simply an instrument of the Mind. It is the medium of thoughts, the force that manifests thoughts and the substance that composes, maintains and activates all manifes-tations.

The Infinite Mind is a medium of space that

separates and centers all things. It is an insulation that keeps all separate in their individuality, and simultaneously centers each of those things, giving them an Image of the Radiant One. Mind is the medium by which thought is carried from one point to another. A medium of transference is required for anything that moves, whether it be of Vibration or matter in order to travel from place to place.

Everything one creates must originate as thought, which consists of vibratory reflections under control of their portion of the All-Mind. If enough Conscious Minds unite, since these, being personalities, are inherently stronger in unison, then they can influence the All-Mind. So, the further we pursue it, the more we can express of it. None can penetrate into and direct the Universal Mind beyond their own acquired capability, which is all the Creator can do for us.

F   "The All-Mind has five separate levels of existence. In order and function, they are:

(a) *Unifier* is the highest state, the level at which all matter in the Universe is in rapport with the combined All-Mind. This level is the one in which every existent thing is united with every other.

(b) *Ultraconscious* is the vehicle for parapsychic functions. It is controlled directly by both the Conscious and the All-Mind. It is the Conscious Direct Link with the Universe, of matter, energy, space, and time.

(c) *Conscious* is the awakened mind, the information-gatherer for the whole mind. Through it the basic senses relay their impressions to the other levels. It is also the Control Center.

(d) *Subconscious* is the area where information is stored until at such time as it is filed in the Unconscious. It also serves to collect knowledge from the Unconscious on command from the Conscious Mind.

(e) *Unconscious* is the part in which dreams are formed. It also serves as the memory bank of the Mind. It acts as a Veil, which protects us by preventing previous embodiment memories from influencing the Conscious Mind, thus altering the present course of Life."

K2   "Man and Woman as one, is the All-Mind's most perfect Creation, in the most desirable Image for Its expression. When this perfect Image of Unity contacts the Mind of the Absolute at work, they find that Magnetic Resonance is the most powerful avenue to greet the active Creator. Unlimited energy is constantly manifesting in all there is, through the action of Universal Mind. Otherwise, It is at rest, in perfect balance, at a center point, or Source of All That IS. This is the Great Mind that created the Universe for the divine, magnetic, and spiritual beings that inhabit the Cosmos in the Divine Image of God."

We have the ability to think and choose of ourselves, but the All-Mind we function within is a Universal Being, that is all of us.

*   *   *

7.
HARMONY

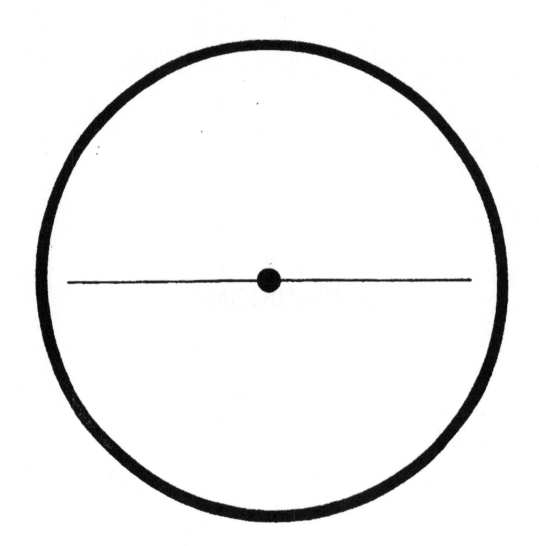

HARMONY

From
UNIVERSAL CONCERTO
By Tuella

Number	Symbol	Law	Color	Tone
7.	⊖	Harmony	Orange	D

4   "Harmony is the balance of all action and penetration of the Force of Creation."

PRINCIPLE

Harmony is to do all things in moderation, in order to arrive at a point of equilibrium where we will be able to know what must be done to progress. Through seeking this balance point within us, we develop the God responsibility within us and no other. Only from within this point of us can we know that which is truth timeless, at that time necessary for our experience. The ability to recognize what is real (discernment) depends upon the ability to maintain balance of being in all phases.

THREE PHASES

1. The Cosmos was built by and upon the principles of Harmony (music), system (arithmetic), and balance (geometry). All law and order evolved out of chaos throughout the Universe, then all things were created.

2. We must at all times try to be in Harmony with each other. The purpose in our being on Earth is to bring about a balance in ourselves, among each other, and with the planet. This can only be achieved through actions of understanding.

3. In Nature, forms blend with others for which they have an Attraction, and Harmony results. To divide these combinations, denying them their natural opposites, and forcing together forms that have no Attraction for one another, results in their exerting all

individual power to divide and seek those opposites. These unbalanced forms seeking to balance themselves would bring about destruction, both from the force of their division and the aftereffects on balanced forms.

Harmony in all that is and shall be, is the perfect state of being, as the Creator wills it. Disharmony of chaos and disorder is the Reaction of discord in Action, and is contrary to Nature, which Itself is Life Eternal. Those who strike a discordant note with the Harmony around them isolate themselves entirely from the vibratory pulse of the Creative Spirit.

As portal vortices of Life Force, we are outlets for the Infinite One, which is constantly seeking to create through us. When we flow in Harmony with All Life, happiness, health, and the abundance of every perfect thing is ours. But create a barrier to the power of Life and we suffer tension, illness, and eventually, destruction.

It is intended that all created forms express Harmoniously together. Each should feel itself through the manifestation of another. Therefore, the manner of growth fills their interest and intensifies a desire for fulfillment. A pattern gradually becomes manifest to all others. Regardless of where service through creation appears, each blends with every other, with joy for the opportunity to serve.

3   "The Universe is one of Order in all things created by Laws and upon a Plan of Evolution. Order in all things brought about Harmony. Harmony is the fruit of all things being done within the Will of God, and according to Divine Plan. The Harmony of Order within the Plan flows down through every Dimension, every level, and every phase of all Nature.

Harmony is Peace, Balance and Protection as it manifests in Cosmos. All phases of Creation are protected by Harmony and order. To bring about chaos in any of these would result in eventual or immediate disharmony, which is destruction and even annihilation. Harmony must be observed and understood at every level of Creation to be appreciated, and then adopted in order to progress at all."

4   "Harmony is the perfect balance of all Creative Force, united into one Vibration. When we come to realize our Oneness with all of Creation, we are then in total Harmony with its Creator. Harmony is, in essence, attunement with the Whole. Cooperation with the Laws of the Universe is Harmony in Action." Live, move and act in conscious awareness of Life, Light and Love, knowing that by doing so, we are keeping our Lives in Divine and Perfect Order.

We must attune all our senses to work together as a Unit of Harmony, in order to fulfill our true purpose in Life. Coordination is the alignment of that which is vital to the whole for perfect expression. Therefore, it is essential that we coordinate our lives in the Laws of Life.

*   *   *

8.
DIMENSIONS

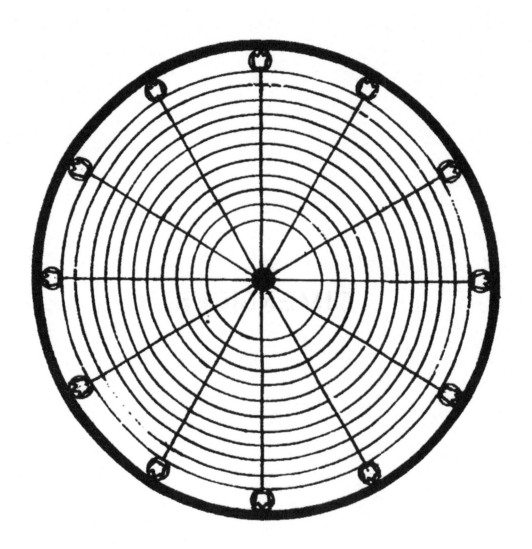

DIMENSIONS
(The Twelve Regents)

From
UNIVERSAL CONCERTO
By Tuella

(The twelve A's with their twelve counterpoint [countapoints] represent the four and twenty Elders, sounding through the four harmonies of F, A minor, V7 and G7. These four movements represent the Eternal Vigilance at the Four Gates of our Universe, three Galaxies to each Gate, at the north, the south, the east and the west.)

Number	Symbol	Law	Color	Tone
8.	✸	Dimensions	Red-Orange	D^b

"Within Creation there is a series of consecutive Dimensions of existence."

PRINCIPLE

A series of planes or levels of manifestation can and does exist when there is an alternating vibration of Light between. There is nothing in the totality of Reality that does not have several corresponding levels or functions. These various functions are the balance between every dimension and are very precisely attuned to one another as facets of Creation.

Nothing remains constant and unchanging. Everything must either advance to a higher level or regress back to a more primitive one.

THREE PHASES

1. In the Primary Cause of Creation, all is perfect. That portion of the whole, manifest as spirit, may become equal with the Creator. To reach that position, it must pass through all stages of development in order to become one with the Source.

2. Throughout the worlds of the Cosmos are many types of spiritual and physical evolutions. Each form of intelligent Life adapts itself to the physical conditions prevalent upon its planet. Most of these evolutions exist in more highly attenuated forms of matter than upon Earth.

3. The vibratory level of energy and matter can be raised or lowered as different

frequency levels occupying the same space
without interfering with each other in any way.
Like radio waves on different bands of the
spectrum they can, and do, coexist in an intra-
dimensional state.

Consider a series of twelve concentric
transparent spheres, one within another (see
symbol on page 126). The count begins with the
central sphere of one, and moves outward to the
sphere of twelve. Each sphere is free to ro-
tate one within and outside of another. There
is no unoccupied space between them. Each
sphere has its own specific Vibration rate and
on each one there is a grid system of corresponding vortex points. Any given vortex on
the outside of each sphere, as a Dimension,
has a corresponding vortex to it on its inside.
This applies through all the concentric Dimensions.

When one desires to shift from Dimension
three to four (outside or inside), and so on,
to any other, they simply change their Vibration accordingly. The person then will be
located in a new place; *tuned in* to objects,
colors and sounds of their surroundings. When
individual perceptions are tuned out of the
environment, they would disappear only to be
replaced by those of another Dimension. Unless the change was done in a state of balance, an imbalance could destroy the person
attempting the shift.

The factor of time has no meaning, as there
is no crossing of space in this transfer process. A change of vibratory rate is equal to
a change of location. This is made possible
by varying the standing waves of the personal
energy field of one's atomic structure. Each
atom of the human body has its own particular
vibration in a permanent state. All operate

and are maintained by a common set of principles.

There are twelve basic Dimensions of existence that are distinguished by varying rates of Vibration, as states of consciousness. These Dimensions are known as: Physical, 1-3; Mental, 4-6; Spiritual, 7-9; and Universal, 10-12. Each plane interpenetrates another region. In the higher octaves of Light, there are no existing individualized aspects of personality such as we know.

Our galactic system is subdivided into twelve segments and Dimensions, each of which has a governing body designed to assist those within its given influence to grow and develop, so that they may move on to another. The term *Dimensions* is synonymous with *Principalities*, which might better explain the character of this process and system of government in fulfilling the Evolutionary Plan of Life. Within each Dimension there are levels, similar to the passage of our solar system through the twelve constellations.

G   "Individual change for adaptation on higher Dimensions is achieved in three aspects, as a cumulative unit effect: (a) live sensibly and positively; (b) raise the level of Conscious awareness; and (c) increase the individual vibratory rate."

*   *   *

9.
LOVE

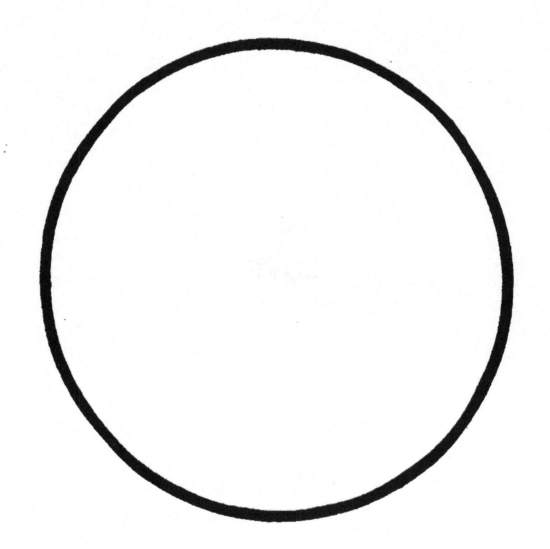

LOVE

Theme

From
UNIVERSAL CONCERTO
By Tuella

The musical pattern above is the all encompassing Universal Theme.

It is both the introductory passage and the closing finale, as well as the recurrent strain that weaves between the other twelve patterns as the intermediary modulation, unifying the whole.

As Love is the outer rim of the Master Symbol enfolding all other components, Love as the Spiritual Essence of Creation, is that Divine Adhesive which binds together All That Is.

-Tuella

Number	Symbol	Law	Color	Tone
9.	◯	Love	Red or Pink	C

"Love is the binding energy of the Universe."

PRINCIPLE

Love causes mutual Attraction. It is the force that protects all Life by keeping it well ordered and secure. Love serves the Will of God by cooperating with it non-destructively. Love is the fulfilling of the Law. It is a kind of cohesion that holds and keeps all things together and in their correct relationship to the Source.

The presence of Love is known through rhythm and Harmony, which keeps all things in order. The presence of hatred is known through chaos and confusion, which keeps all things in disorder. It is by our use of Love that we are able to bring order and constructive results into our Lives. *Love is the great negative. It is the Issue, or God of all Creation.*

THREE PHASES

1. To work in Harmony with our Divine Spirit is to be Conscious of Love in our being. Love is a radiation from the heart of Deity through all Creation, and especially through us toward all other forms, without division of any kind.

2. Unity of purpose and existence cannot be conceived without the root of Love for all. As our minds develop in understanding, we become aware that only through cooperation with others and the spiritual Love of the One Infinite Intelligence and Power, can we effectively

improve the conditions of personal daily life.

3. Love is an all-encompassing force which brings about the Creation of everything. It is the Attraction that brings all beings together in the act of Creation, thereby perpetuating the race. The Creator never can, nor ever does, give forth *anything* but Love.

The Circle symbolizes Eternal Love and Union. Love is the circle of all Manifestation. Love is sacred and spiritual, for a person or persons. A spiritual Love expresses through that one small spark of the Infinite Spirit present within each of us. This is an impersonal Love expressed to All. Love is the *conscious* thought of oneness towards all things. In Love all live and move and have their being. Eventually all will recognize their basic unity of being, when one is for another honestly, sincerely, and not selfishly against oneself.

All that is transcendent, beautiful, and perfect is Natural and according to the Law of Love. Anything other than this is sub-natural. When we choose to look away from our Source of Love as the plan by which to live, a condition of misery follows. When we look away from Love, we are deliberately and *consciously choosing* the experience of chaos. Those who seek to exist without Love cannot survive long anywhere in Creation. Such an effort is bound to bring failure, sadness, and dissolution.

The truth of Harmonious Love is the only real authority. Each living being is united with their fellow beings. Nothing exists without this union. To hate anything or anyone dissolves unity and produces discord, which is the incorrect blend of the components of Love, produced by imbalanced thought. The absence of thinking in this manner produces a condition without hatred.

One must Love the Creative Spirit, who is our neighbor manifested in individualized form. Unconditional Love is releasing each and everyone to remain near, or take another path different from our own. Love is understanding throughout the Universe; it is the constant of all worlds. Love is infinite freedom, selflessness and not the carnality which is often mistaken for Love. It brings forth peace within its experience. Where Love is felt, the complete Power of the Source then manifests.

Love is stronger than Life and deeper than the boundless depths of time and space. The sexual instinct, when motivated by Love, altruism and unselfishness, is no more erroneous than any other desire. But in the higher spiritual worlds it is nonexistent. Instead, they embrace as one being, enfolding in a unity of the spirit, untouched by sensuality. The embrace of spirit is shared by all of those in the Light of God's Infinite Love throughout the entire Universe. All boundaries of self are lost in a unity of being.

*   *   *

10.
POLARITY

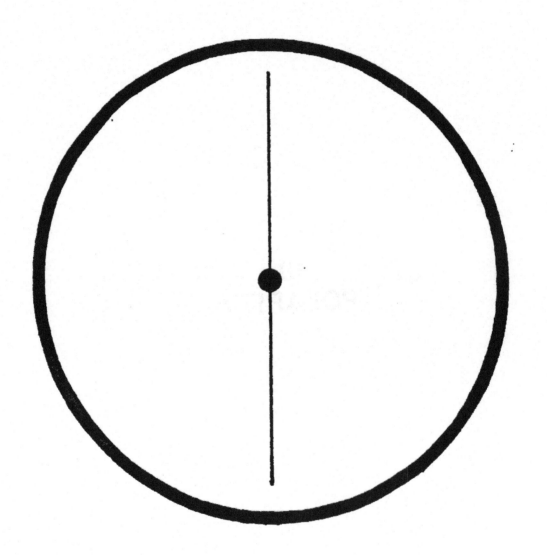

POLARITY

From
UNIVERSAL CONCERTO
By Tuella

Number	Symbol	Law	Color	Tone
10.	⊕	Polarity	Red-Purple	c^b

"Polarity requires that two equal and opposite, positive and negative poles of force be active in order to manifest action as the resultant."

PRINCIPLE

In Nature, the positive and negative poles are brought together in relationship, resulting in an effect—the offspring—allowing for the continuance of all Life. Within this form, which was the product of union, is contained a certain portion of the original two primal forces. Therefore, one plus one equals three. Positive and negative are coexisting poles, each dependent on the other, for one would have no existence without the other.

THREE PHASES

1. In spirit, like attracts like. The polarity of an intention draws a like experience in our Lives. Positive is a higher and less visible, or felt, vibration, and therefore is termed more spiritual. The Creator is not a solid substance.

2. The finite mind can unfold itself into the Infinite by polarity union and balance. When combined, these two polarities comprise all existence, both known and unknown. We create our reality, from the viewpoint of neutral energy.

3. In the physical and emotional levels opposites attrace each other. Negative is a lower vibration and is the most material make-up in existence.

God has the power to keep unlike things apart and, by induction, allow union between polarities of equal opposition.

The entire concept of proper mating is to bring out the best possible expression in both persons. Together they should blend spiritually and mentally, but emotionally and physically complement each other as a perfect unit of expression. Union and mating is a mechanism for the fullest expression of soul, social, and biological development. It is a means of stimulating creativeness and progress.

To form a union and not fulfill natural mating requirements, the two individuals would be antagonistic, resentful, lack in creative interest in Life, and contribute little to the union, themselves, or their fellow being. This would constitute an incompatible union, and later on, a complete separation would of necessity follow, or end in destruction of both.

One should learn to select a mate: First, by spiritual attunement; second, by mental pursuits and like interests; and third, by emotional complements. We need not learn the fourth, for physical Attraction of opposites is always in operation on the material level. Mates should be chosen by a Universal Awareness of a perfect and complete union on all levels of spiritual, mental, emotional, and physical development.

The sexual expression of procreation is one of the highest expressions of God, in that it takes in the sense of touch. It is an expression of two beings, perfectly combined in all areas, combined as one. Two persons, when perfectly mated, stay together as long as their desire and mutual progress continue--sometimes for many lifetimes.

MAN was first androgynous, combining male and female as one, as the Image of God. The male and female came into being as a result of the separation of MAN into positive and negative forces. In man, the positive and active was expressed and the negative suppressed. In woman, the negative and receptive was expressed and the positive suppressed. These forms were created to assist one another in the struggle for at-one-ment with the Creative Spirit.

Every form is composed of definite measurements of space, surrounded by active particles of force. All substance is made up of these tiny units, called *atoms*. An atom may be compared to a miniature solar system containing a central sun (nucleus) of positive charge, around which, in specific orbits, revolve twelve planets (electrons) of negative charges. The solar electrical charge equals perfectly the total number of planetary electrical charges revolving about it, thus forming a single unit of force.

4   "Polarity is the combined force of positive and negative which produces the flow of Creative Power. It consists of two equal and opposite halves united into the Whole. It is the blending of opposites in perfect union with the Whole, which produces perfect flow of Divine Nature."

*   *   *

11.
ATTRACTION

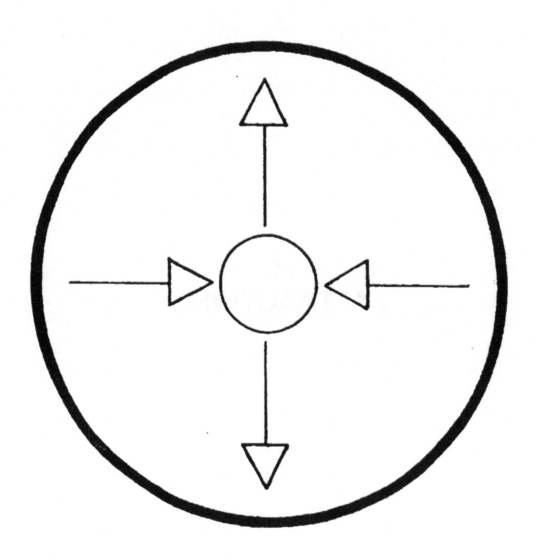

ATTRACTION

From
UNIVERSAL CONCERTO
By Tuella

Number	Symbol	Law	Color	Tone
11.	. ⊕	Attraction	Purple	B

"As like poles repel each other, unlike poles have an Attraction."

PRINCIPLE

Just as the north pole of a magnet will attract the south pole of another magnet, so the electrons attract the protons. Similar poles of magnets repel each other, and so do similar charges of electricity. Likes repel and unlikes attract. Attraction and its opposite, repulsion, are the forces used to create or destroy something in our Universe. Without Attraction and repulsion there can be no movement, and therefore, no Life. "Attraction is the pulling together force of the center of all opposite polarities."

THREE PHASES

1. On the spiritual level, like attracts like. This means that a positive force will always repel a negative force. Whatever we project attracts a similar energy. Attraction of mind and spirit constantly exerts a pressure up, and inward toward the center, to the fold from where we started through the planets and systems of progression.

2. We have the ability and the power to Attract to ourselves all that we *want*, and we have the power to repel that which we *do not want*. Thoughts are forms of Life Force. Each one has its distinct frequency; therefore, all those which are attuned to the same vibratory rate and wavelength contain similar aspects, attracting one another.

3. Attraction on the physical plane tends to hold an object together. Everything in the Universe exists because of the power of Attraction. "It is a force that ingathers, that tends to coherence, adhesion, and absorption. Attraction is that which results in the coalescence of Manifestation. Disintegration is its opposite expression, having effected that which makes cohesion possible."

4

All operates throughout the Cosmos by Attraction and Repulsion. Each are interconnected as a unit of force within the self-sustaining Vortex of the Whole. Unlike poles Attract each other to become a unit; in turn, it will Attract another to become a large unit, and so on. Like poles repel each other, seeking not to come together. It is where units tend to remain separate from one another. The balance between Attraction and Repulsion causes the rotation and orbit of many units about the Center of Force, as planets (electrons) around the sun (nucleus) as a complete system. Everything without exception, from the smallest to the largest in the Whole, that is Creation, is contained within a Vortex in a constant state of field rotation of force created by the Mind Force of the Universe.

All material forms of Manifestation must, by progression, return to their Original Source, by conversion from one state of being to another. All objects of matter are made perishable by the stress between units of force which formed them. All forms, on every plane, were created by the external influence of Attraction and Repulsion upon the flow of Central Force, which has been slowed down to a very low level of Vibration. The pure power out of which matter was created is constantly straining to break free from the binding force of Magnetic Resonance and return to its original gaseous state.

4   "Attraction (or Affinity) is related to polarization, motion and propulsion. It pulls to the neutral center that which is negative to that center which is the point of neutrality, oneness and Harmony. It is always in operation, manifesting in regulated Divine Order and rhythm. Attraction is the flow, or pulse of the Universe and the beat of the heart of God. Within Oneness there is no polarity, there is only unity and Harmony. Only in the pulling away of repulsion does separation take place. Between the counter points of Attraction and Repulsion, a balanced field exists, which is oneness."

When we, through the Action of our desire, claim something, we Attract it to ourselves. Immediately we set into motion the opposite Law of Repulsion, raising a barrier that repels that which is unlike our request. Attraction always brings to us our own, because we are one with God. God is Infinite in Essence of action, motion, and power, and we are infinite in our ability to control that Power within ourselves. Therefore, we are one with God. With the reality of Attraction in our whole Life, we will become infused with the Power to obtain that which we seek.

*   *   *

12.
MANIFESTATION

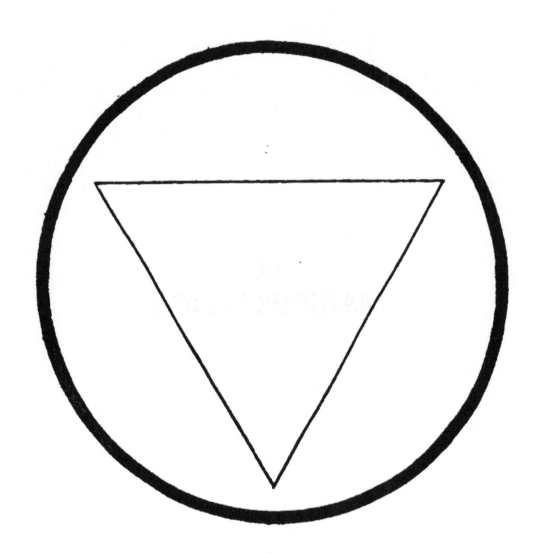

MANIFESTATION

Number	Symbol	Law	Color	Tone
12.	$\bigtriangledown$ (in circle)	Manifesta-tion	Purple-Blue	B^b

"Creation is the result of One Cosmic Mind acting in three phases."

PRINCIPLE

The Creator brought the Universe into Manifestation through the use of the Trinity Force of Life (Will), Light (Intelligence), and Love (Form). Nothing can be manifested without this thought power that the Infinite One used to bring all into being.

Any image which we can conceive (visualize) in action, is in reality. We cannot conceive of something which does not exist. Through the power of creative thought we can consciously select and manifest our reality. A vortex, created by thought force, can attract substance and condense it into various states of matter.

THREE PHASES

1. Father designates the phase which knows and thinks. It activates Creation by thinking ideas to be created, and so instructing.

2. Mother designated the phase of action which manifests the Creation. This is effected by Itself becoming and functioning as the Manifestation.

3. Issue (or God) designates an idea of Creation. Whether or not it be manifested already according to the image is not the process of Creation, for it is in reality created once the Father so decides, and the manifesting necessarily follows.

We are living in a Universe of matter, energy, space, and time, conceived out of Intelligence and perpetuated by Force. The structure of the Whole and everything within it is built on unit creating unit, which in turn creates others, all resulting from One Creative Spirit. Attraction and Repulsion form a unit of energy that brings all into existence. Matter is the final Manifestation of Force that began at a mugh higher, Central Point. Creative Force can only be understood when it is manifest in an effect, as Action and Reaction, within the range of our physical perception, or outside of its limits, in the range of detection by sensitive instruments.

Our contact with the world about us is determined by the range of our senses, and is the basis of all our knowledge concerning it. There are many different frequency levels beyond our range of perception. Each of these planes contains many inhabited planets. Some of these coexist with, or overlap, those visible to us, while others are in seemingly empty space, as is our own world on another level of perception. Each Dimension has its own specific rate of Vibration and wave pattern which we must be on to move in or out of its field of conscious existence. Every plane has its part in the evolution of our inner being.

A physical form is taken on by a spiritual being so that it can come to *know itself* through manifestation. The material plane provides a place which one enters and through introspection, learns of their true spiritual essence. An awareness of that which is to be known can only come after many experiences within forms of one's own making, on several Dimensions. Ultimately, the spirit within becomes experienced and known completely, through comprehending the differences between the transitory nature of matter and the eternal character of the spirit. We, as part of the Eternal Pattern of Life in form, give to the animal substance the ability to express and recognize the spirit.

The Creative Spirit is the Source from which all things began, and is in all Manifestation. The form of Creation is only a channel through which the All Inclusive Life expresses itself. A form that cannot be a channel of Life must be transmuted by gradual stages into a higher elevation of form through which it can, to serve as an expression of spirit. The human body is the consummation of all lesser forms of matter, and is the highest representation of Deity on the physical plane.

4   "Manifestation is the Mind of the Creator bringing forth that which allows an expression of its own Force. Creation begins when the higher forces act to become manifested in the lower Dimensions as matter. The cohesive force of Love is the Balance between the Positive and Negative elements. The Balance between these two forces must exist, in order to maintain existence itself. Imbalance of these Vibrations would disintegrate any manifested form
15 after a relatively brief period." "That which is manifest is the illusion of physical and the unmanifest is the Reality of thought idea which brought it into temporary being."

★   ★   ★

FIVE

THE MASTER SYMBOL

THE MASTER SYMBOL

The Master Symbol is the original key designed to represent the operation of Creation, and our Awareness on twelve levels of Reality, which cannot otherwise be visualized. The concept of the Master Symbol incorporates a sequence of symbolic representations to assist us in achieving a position from which to envision the operation of the Universal Laws. In so displaying them in accordance with specific conditions, we can remove the thought barriers created by the arbitrary interpretations which we may have concerning the concept of Reality.

10 "The simplified version of the circle enveloping the cross, known as the Solar Cross, is incomplete. We are now desiring to release a more complete and complex version, as the Master Symbol of the Universe. In its entire form, the symbol will correlate the four important aspects of Source, Laws, Energies, and Divisions into One Whole.

"Each single component as it applies to the separate Laws, is a familiar diagram to most of you, as they are viewed singularly. The objective before us now is that you might see how they all incorporate to create the Whole. This is the outer purpose for the Master

Symbol, which is also the symbol of Mastery, as well as the Master's Symbol."

7   "We are endeavoring to speak to the world through twelve symbols combined to create the Master Symbol. We can communicate with the inner consciousness and soul memory more satisfactorily in this manner than we could with many words, that most would not understand. The study of the symbol is a *subconscious activity*, and the study of words is a *conscious activity*. That is, the symbol will reveal on inner levels the principles that are involved, and words will reveal on outer levels the causes and effects that are involved.

"We desire to place the Master Symbol before humanity with an awareness of its components, as they spiritually apply on all levels. The Cosmic Self of each individual will embody the symbol within the innermost levels of being, and use it during meditation to trigger memory and understanding on the conscious level. This Master Symbol within will awaken dormant awareness within, just as its simple counterpart, the Solar Cross, has already done."

14   "This composite symbol of Law was designed and intended to be used as a teaching and awakening tool. The Master Symbol is comparable to a book containing a great amount of factual information, but the student must learn its language in order to appreciate and comprehend it. The Center and the Laws are the keys that unlock the language of this composite form. It represents twelve levels of Cosmic Awareness within you, as an integrating expression of energy with all forms of activity."

15   "The Master Symbol and its parts are already recorded within the subconscious of all those

who have passed through the training periods of
Etheria, before embodiment.   The intention is
to now pull this information through the human
consciousness in a way that will assist all
people in understanding the Creative Source,
and their relationship to It.   This definite
union must consciously be known and strength-
ened. Through the application of the Master
Symbol of Creation, the students will lift up
their eyes to a Greater Picture of the Magnif-
icence of all Worlds and the Unity of all beings under these Great Divine Laws."

14   "All inclusive is the basic interrelating
principle, wherein there is an essential unity
between oneself and the various forces of Nature. The Universal Laws governing your mind
and body reflect and partake of the harmonious
function with Nature as a Whole. When one
perceives of himself as a microcosm, his way
of Life takes on the character of the macro-
cosmic order of the Whole. The Law Symbol system exists to assist, recover, maintain, and
develop a Natural Way of Life for All.

        "The mind can realize and integrate the
twelve parts of this system, as a guide toward
a conscious self-sustaining Life. The symbols
contained within the composite pattern were
created through converting the Power of the
Source into separate images. By a reciprocal
process, they can release a system so struc-
tured in its form as to define the processes
of Nature as a set of interrelationships unified into One Whole."

7   "The objective of the study of Law Symbol
Concepts is to allow the inner level of consciousness to understand, rather than to ap-
peal to the reasoning intellect. Many will
read without an outward comprehension, but the
simple symbols themselves, when meditated upon,

will work from within, even as the body sleeps. Study of the symbols, along with the words of explanation, should be sufficient to enlighten an understanding of these Laws."

4   "The component symbols represent the over-all basic principles contained in the Master Symbol. We need to let the pattern unfold of its own flow and then flow with it as we go. Within the design of this symbol will be the silent message of the All Creative Principle and Primary Cause. The Universal Laws are everything to us--our existence, mission, and service to God within the Greater Whole."

8   "You will find a realization on conscious levels of a knowledge already placed within you eons ago. You carry in the inner recesses of being, an understanding of the Universal Laws, that were once applied even on this planet somewhat, though not as strongly as upon the other planets which you originally volunteered from. This is within your soul and always will be, as you continue to strive to demonstrate its virtually unlimited applications on conscious levels.

"There is always more knowledge within your inner level of being than can be brought forth and applied on this planet, or plane. Nevertheless, portions of this knowledge will yet be applied. Remember, that because the present civilization is out of step with the Universal Laws, much of what you may know will not be applied until planet Earth is renewed.

"The Master Symbol is, in essence, the Symbol of All Reality, for without its existing components as Laws of Force, there would be no Reality. When you study the symbol, you are perceiving ALL THAT IS."

5   "The understanding, operation, and control
of the Forces of the Universe are all intri-
cately interwoven in the visualization of the
Master Symbol. Make no mistake about it, with
this symbol and a comprehension of it, planets
can be either created or destroyed. As you
work with the Symbol, it will work with you.
The Laws, as symbols, represent the regulated
powers within all things. The Master Symbol
is the composite of all forces present in the
Cosmos, superimposed upon one another as One
Force."

15   "The Master Symbol of Creation will perpetuate motion. As Life, it will Resonate Magnetism wherever it is. It is an instrument of
Light. It reverberates Love on this plane.
It is the Manifestation of Universal Law within
our Octave. In balancing the mental activity
of all, it brings Polarity to Being. It reflects below that which is above, revealing
the Action and Reaction of Cause and Will.
Therefore, it will have its own effect upon
the planet. It carries its own individual Vibration that is living, moving, influencing,
and bringing Life, from out of its own Vortex."

This Wheel of Law, Truth and Life symbolizes
the way of escape from the illusory world
toward the Center. The one who has attained
the Central Point of the Wheel and remains
bound to the unvarying mean, in indissoluble
union with the Origin, partaking of its immut-
ability and unseen activity, will be secure in
repose. To return to the root is to enter into
the state of unity; that is, to throw off the
bonds of things transitory and contingent.

Reality is the realm in which a state of
existence is unfolded, comprising many component parts adhering together. The totality of
the manifest is as a reflection of permanent

creative activity. To leave the circumference
for the center is equivalent to moving from the
exterior to the interior, from form to contem-
plation, from division to unity, from space to
spacelessness, and from time to timelessness.

The purpose of the Master Symbol is to
Awaken an Awareness within us by conveying certain information and experiences which act as
a Key, unlocking and removing the barriers between our conscious and subconscious brain. As
a result, an essential link which connects with
our Creator is re-forged. A definite factor
in this possibility is the integration of our
nervous system and the emotional and physical
centers of the brain. This is achieved through
a sequence of symbol alignment with our higher
being. This composite symbol requires an open,
inductive frame of Mind, with a desire to Attract specific memory patterns, to be effective.

Step by step, we will show how one Law and
its Symbol superimpose upon the others that
have gone before, building up the composite
until it is seen as the one Whole Unit of the
Master Symbol.   In order for there to be an
effective and complete understanding of the
Universal Laws, the Number, Symbol, Color, and
Tone for each one must be interpreted in a perfect state of meditative balance, so that the
subconscious, conscious and ultraconscious levels of Mind can function as one. At first this
may be difficult, but as we discipline both the
body and the mind with practice, success will
be ultimately achieved. Consider focusing at-
tention upon the Whole, as a self-integrating
and sustaining system, formed by the interdependent relationships of the Laws.

15   "Through your involvement with the associa-
        tior of each Symbol, Law and Principle, you

will be able to key into the subconscious,
and an awakening will take place. Produc-
ive thinking will be the result, when using
them as a Meditative Exercise. Sit with a
blank piece or pad of paper and a pencil or
pen before you, then draw one symbol component at a time, beginning with the Source
Center, while at the same time visualizing
its activity of meaning. When ready to pass
on to the next symbol, pause and clear your
mind. Proceed, then, in the order in which
the symbols follow, so that you may experience
the entire process and pattern of the Master
Symbol of Creation."

                    *   *   *

0. CENTRAL FORCE

Symbol

Principle

4   "Central Force is the Primary Energy of the Center Core of All Creation. It is the One Source from which all other cause power manifests as Cosmic Events. Central Force is the Origin, or Beginning Power, which gives Creation its eternal and infinite existence. One starts in all things from the Center and Source of all Life, which is formless.

"The One Unit of Almighty Cause is blended together within the Center, without actual division of any kind. This is the Heart of Divine Will. The principles of Creation go forth and return as forces linked to this common Center of Primal Cause. The Center is the Nameless Reality of Creation."

Central Force is the pivotal point about which the Laws of Nature become manifest, as twelve aspects of power. Each Law has its own unique identity concept, manifesting itself as a secondary energy having definite characteristics given to it by the Creative Spirit. All parts cooperate as a Whole, through an interdependent relationship, establishing a continual pattern of purpose. A dot within a circle represents the Infinite Being, One, and All in All.

Symbol   1. *LIFE*   Composite

Principle

4   "Life is a rotating energy of cosmic rays.
It is ever in motion throughout Creation. The
Central Force curves outward in a circular motion, that manifests as Four Forces enveloping
everything with Life. Life, as the All Inclusive Intelligence, is present throughout the
Whole, in varying combinations of Force and
Form. A cross in the form of two overlapping
sine curves represents the Divine Omnipresence
through the whirling Action of the Four Great
Forces."

Symbol   2.   *MAGNETIC RESONANCE*   Composite

Principle

2   "Magnetic Resonance is the medium for the
transference of Creative Thought Force, from
one level or point to another. It is the force
out of which all things are formed and held in
space. Magnetic Resonance is the power of Life
present in everything. It perpetuates the activity of the Life Force throughout the Cosmic
Universe. Three waves that are parallel to
one another represent the cooperative union
of the Trinity Phase of Magnetism."

Symbol   3. *ACTION AND
                  REACTION*   Composite

Principle

Action and Reaction are the means by which
the imperceptible Central Force is converted
to manifest as different forms of power. The
Primary Flow of Creative Thought which permeates all space is so high in Vibration that
it is the unmanifest Cause of all Effects in
the Universe. We create, develop, and transform our environment, and in turn, our experiences within it, by the Action and Reaction of
our Thought Force, or concept of Reality.

Symbol   4. *VIBRATION*   Composite

Principle

4   "Vibration is the flowing movement of the
pulsating Life Force through all things. It
governs everything within the entire Universe.
Vibration is energy and you change the energy
to change the mass. It forms a portal into
density and out again, through adjustment of
its individual frequency. A vortex represents
a standing rotary wave of motion that manifests
within and between mediums of matter, energy,
space, and time, as a density of existence."

<u>Symbol</u>   5.   *LIGHT*   <u>Composite</u>

Principle

14   "Light is one of the most potent forces in
all the Creation. It is capable of expression
in many forms. Light transcends all forms of
matter Vibration, until it returns back to its
Source, the Radiant One. All Creative Thoughts
are reflected in the Light, known as an aura.
When we acknowledge the Light of the Infinite
One in everything, we are showing recognition
of the Source. Beyond Creation is only a consciousness of Light."

<u>Symbol</u>   6.   *MIND*   <u>Composite</u>

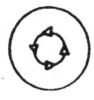

Principle

Mind is that which continues forever through
all Dimensions of progress, into the unmanifest
state. It is omnipresent, and acts upon all.
All exists within Mind, for God is Infinite.
All within Creation is linked by its access to
the Central Force of Mind, which flows throughout all planes of being. Time and space are
limitless in Mind, as these are its creations.
Mind consists of five levels of consciousness,
directing the Creative Forces of Reality as
one conscious unit.

Symbol   7.   *HARMONY*   Composite

Principle

3   "Harmony is order and balance of the whole.
It is health and perfection. Harmony within
one's being is the stillness of peace. It is
compatibility between two like poles of equal
spiritual force. When oneness is achieved with
all Creation, one is in total Harmony with it
and its Source.   Oneness with the Creative
Source is Power. Harmony within each part of
the Whole is achieved through cooperative service and mutual benefit."

Symbol   8.   *DIMENSIONS*   Composite

Principle

3   "Within Creation there is a series of twelve
hierarchal forms of conscious evolution and
responsibility. When one is aware of this government, one is quite willing to participate
and serve on whatever level is required by
him, to ascend.   In this way all are evolving
toward a condition in which all are serving
equally within the Whole. Each Dimension
exists to provide a stage for the development
of spirit toward union with the Source."

Symbol   9.   *LOVE*   Composite

Principle

Love is the return to unity from division.
It is the eternal portion of Life given to
each soul from the Infinite Spirit. Love is
the relationship between the Creator and all
created. It is the whole reason for the manifestation of all within Creation. Love is a
conscious oneness with all Creation. It is
the binding energy which holds everything together. Love is the perfect state of eternity.
A circle represents unity of all.

Symbol   10.   *POLARITY*   Composite

Principle

Polarity is a unit of equal force consisting of one positive (active) and one negative
(passive) pole. The varying proportions of
these two modes of force characterize Creation.
When they polarize, a spiral motion is formed,
which constructs a galaxy, or atom, and later
returns it to the original unmanifested condition. The quantity of power distributed
throughout the Universe is invariable. A circle divided into two equal sections by a line
represents the bipolar force.

Symbol   11. *ATTRACTION*   Composite

Principle

Attraction and Repulsion are the two fields
of Action of Primary Energy. These are transformed into the power which pervades the Universe. Energy is only recognized by the effect
of its Actions. When seen in operation, Attraction balances the inertial forces, bringing Harmony to all Creation. Attraction and Repulsion
are the forces used in the creation, maintenance
and destruction of all things within the Cosmos.

Symbol   12. *MANIFESTATION*   Composite

Principle

Manifestation is the result of sensing a
constant rate of a particular amount of radiation, in the form of any surrounding environment, condition, or state of reality. Every
form that expresses Life is a channel of individualized spirit that manifests itself through
Vibratory impulses of thought, color and sound,
that can be sensed, known, and intuited. Our
divinity is the complete nature of what our
Creative Spirit is manifesting through us.

J

"Within Section Four, the Universal Laws, a corresponding musical pattern accompanies each of the individual symbols of the Master Symbol of the Solar Cross. These channeled musical patterns are individually based upon a mathematical number and formula corresponding to each symbol. The inspired melodies, as technically presented, reveal the mathematical structure of the symbol with each interpretation.

"A student, combining Meditation upon both the visual symbol and the audible musical pattern, will receive an inner response producing association of both aids, with either one eventually leading to the same results on inner levels.

"The complete musical presentation consists of thirteen patterns, representing the Source, and the twelve Universal Laws. A full sheet and cassette recording music rendition of 'The Universal Concerto' is planned for later release, as time permits, weaving all of the patterns into a completely interpreted musical score.

4   "The Master Symbol as it appears in various places, either on the front cover or within the text, is a near replica to the one in our Hall of Higher Laws. It will accomplish its purpose in the Minds of souls who use it. I ordain this, *The Master Symbol of Universal Law*, as built upon the former symbol of the Solar Cross. The world will know it as the Master Symbol of the Solar Cross, but in time, it will come to be known as above."

The spirit of God is the Sum of All Creative Principle in the Universe. Everything in Creation exists because of these Laws. God is the ultimate combination of all the powers and

abilities used in the Cosmos, the Sum Total.
Everything has its own particular pattern
within the Whole. Most of the acts of Creation by the Infinite One were done through the
concentrated Power of His twelve Laws, controlled by the All Mind.

The individual symbols illustrate the actual
working of the Law. They also show the results when applying them. When the twelve Universal Laws are used in a combined state, with
their principle forces in unity on any purpose,
that task will be accomplished. As Creative
Spirit, we Attract Power to ourselves, convert
and direct it, thereby creating our reality.
We coexist and create as a collective Whole,
with our Source, because we were created in the
image and likeness of our Source. Creation is
represented by the Master Symbol of Universal
Law.

★ ★ ★

SIX

THE GREAT AWAKENING

THE GREAT AWAKENING

All beings, worlds, planes, and dimensions are in an eternal process toward Absolute Perfection. This process develops within the Divine Plan so as to give everyone, without exception, the opportunities of multiple periods of existence that the long journey throughout the entire Universe requires to finally ascend or evolve upon the dimensions of Conscious Awareness and Service of Life. In the Integral Universe everything evolves from the simplest forms to those levels of existence which are more complicated and advanced. In all worlds, planes, and dimensions of Nature, this Great Awakening is fulfilled: "As it is Above, so it is Below."

Every spirit has many thousands of years (incarnations) for slow physiological and psychological development that gradually changes the whole being so it may acquire knowledge which will later be conveyed into abilities. These develop from the simplest ways of thinking, assimilating experiences and changing progressive goals up to advanced social levels of organization. These abilities transform him into a cultured, improved, experienced inhabitant of the world, who is constantly raising his standard of living by acquiring knowledge and understanding necessary to accomplish his goals and desires.

This galactic system teems with life and intelligence, in every direction and in all states of development. There are a few newer planetary systems within which the development is only approaching the Stone Age, and a little beyond. We are upon a planet within such a system—therefore, one of the least developed of the races of planetary life. There are races slightly in advance of ours who live in city-type space ships with controlled environments, free of any planet. Still, there are races who are much farther ahead in development that are pure intelligence. We would not recognize them as living beings at all, by our standards.

The Universe functions as a whole, with all dimensions coexisting with each other. A plane or region of space is divided into various levels, distinct states, or conditions in the development of primal cosmic energy and matter. According to the gradations in vibrations and wavelengths, and in the type of forces that manifest themselves in these states, they correspond to a certain level of life. Absolute free will choice in thoughts and actions only operates on the proving grounds—or planets—of which the earth is one. Beyond the fourth dimension, however, the Guardians of Evolution supervise and control the spirit's development.

The Universal Laws of Progressive Evolution form the fundamental basis of all growth. These cosmic principles and forces take part in this great evolutionary process. All spirits experience growth on their long journey from the primitive to perfection. There are many areas of knowledge and skills yet to be explored, that are necessary for a satisfactory or advanced state of Life unlimited. The length of time required to reach Absolute Perfection depends upon the complexity of education, understanding and application of this knowledge to the achievement of certain spiritual goals. Each experience of *applied* understanding improves the entire being. Ignorance blocks the path of comprehension.

Throughout time, some of us have incarnated into the vibration of Earth from other planets, planes, and dimensions. Many of us have volunteered an entire lifetime to special missions, to be of service to both this planet and its people. When we, of our own free will, enter this planetary environment, we lose the memory of our origination and our purpose, for the most part. Some are confused; yet, for those who remember, adapting comes easily. Embodiment brings an inner struggle between the knowledge of the task that is before us and the loss of memory, augmenting the task. Our minds eventually generate the necessary frequency of space and time to correlate with this dimension. When the pattern evolves, then we can fulfill our assignment. Only about ten percent remember a portion of memory instruction to accomplish the task.

The Great Awakening involves four basic steps: *1. Seeking; 2. Meditation; 3. Awareness; and 4. Service,* to be explained in sequence.

*   *   *

1. SEEKING

Seeking is the development of our point of view. Each step we advance elevates our Awareness of the Whole.

The Inner Being is saturated with many memories which are held dormant until certain Basic Truths are encountered that activate them. When we are exposed to the Universal Laws, as concepts, we gradually awaken within ourselves *a desire for learning* more about the Universe, our relationship to it, our purpose in Life, where we came from, and our ultimate destiny. When these Cosmic Principles are in proper sequence, many more such memories will gradually surface, and as they are assembled together, form *a definite pattern of an unfolding awareness.*

Seeking is prompted by an inner desire and thought. The Mind is both conscious and subconscious; overlapping them is *Intuition*. *Seeking* is following the Path of Inner Guidance. Some follow the steps to their purpose with conscious recognition; others do so unconsciously. The conscious sense of proper direction in Thought and Action is the trustworthy approach of Guidance.

Seeking is an unfoldment (awakening) of understanding our True Self, the Creative Spirit through Reality, and at the same time, is a freeing of ourselves from hindering circumstances. The intellect has a tendency to create complexities out of things which are otherwise purely simple. Therefore thoughts, not controlled, can create barriers to simple comprehension.

We are blocked from *finding* our true identity and growth until we, of our own free will, seek to know, understand, and adhere to the Universal Laws of Evolution in all phases of Life. As a consequence of adapting to them, we find our growth and development flows easily. Seeking brings change in this manner through our thoughts, actions, and experiences.

Seek the simple way to accomplish that which you desire. Keep complexity to a minimum. The more intense the feeling is within the desire, the more quickly it will be obtained. The desire activates one or more of the Universal Laws at any given moment, and you draw upon their powers, which act through you to the degree you permit and control them. When desire is free from selfishness or curiosity, such will come to you. When it injures another creation in its manifestation, then an equal amount of compensation, through Action and Reaction, will take place at some time in your life. We cannot desire and seek that which is not possible of manifestation somewhere in the Cosmos.

Thought plus Energy in motion (E-motion) equals Creative Thought Force, seeking to manifest its action through some form of reaction. The Force of Reciprocal Attraction drives and unites everything which is similar. Thought originates on the mental level and will, in time, manifest as a complete form on the physical level. Understanding of this Law will enable us to manifest and control other Laws of Creation.

The Mind is the only cause that effects what we see in manifestation. Mind is eternal and supreme intelligence (Light) in the Universe. It is the Vital Force, and only our Creative Thought Patterns can vary this power. When we realize our true relationship to Creation, as being an active part of it, everything that we need and desire is provided.

Seeking results in finding the Truth that is within us. Any erroneous thoughts which interfere with this return to unity must be refused. The mental, emotional, and physical aspects of us appear to be the predominating factors in our lives. They are necessary and useful in their own place and field of expression, but only when these phases of our being are stilled through meditation can we come to *know and experience* more of our Inner Self and of Life.

The conscious mind is the eternal record of our knowing. It is composed of many atoms of different experiences encountered through our progression. When we pass from one density to another, it is necessary to go *within* to reach the true knowledge of our many experiences, derived from a pattern of successive incarnations. The subconscious mind is the storehouse of this memory, independent of the normal functions of the conscious mind.

Seeking is the act of thinking and becoming aware of what already exists, through silencing our own thoughts to allow those of the Creative Intelligence (Light) to fill the void.

*   *   *

2. MEDITATION

Meditation is the act of relaxing and balancing our whole being, through bringing it into attunement.

Reality is within each of us. Our Creator provided within each of us, eternal knowledge and abilities similar to His own, to govern and shape our environment at will. Through the process of meditation we can know it exists—however dormant—waiting to be realized and used properly. It is only necessary that we contact the Source within us, to achieve a state of *unity*, which will gradually allow the Creative Intelligence (Light), and Power (Life) to manifest (Love) through us.

From the center of our being we will *find* the Cause, Essence, and Power of the whole Universe. Let us look into the great *Cause* of all things, and not the Effect. The Mind, being a part of God, is infinite. It is a reservoir of potential energy, of vibrations and wavelengths (of sounds and colors) operating within us, which we have the ability to utilize, as we become aware that we are the most precise synthesizing generators of Power, existing in the body of God.

The objective of meditation is to allow the inner level of our subconscious mind to re-orient and organize the outer level of our conscious mind, so that we might become aware, through our Ultraconscious Mind, of a vaster order and purpose to all life. We can trace back the Master Symbol (blueprint) of Creation, from the physical level to the original thought archetype that still remains in the levels of Creative Thought. The amount of Thought Force exerted on the higher mental levels determines how quickly the transition back from it to the physical level, takes place.

The composite Master Symbol serves as a key of remembrance for those who recognize its significance. By meditating upon it and its sequence of Law Symbols, the Master Symbol will automatically put us into the correct level of mind and vibrational pattern for lifting of the memory veil. The more we meditate upon this symbol, the more we remember.

When colors and sounds (music) are used together within the meditative process, they
D6 raise the Vibration of Attunement. "The display is used by us to untie the mental and physical bodies, or to bring the two bodies in tune so that we can absorb what we see and hear, and more fully understand what is to be presented." Each hue of color corresponds to a tone of sound on the Vibratory Scale, and produces its own specific release of personal energy. Every manifestation, including the Master Symbol of the Solar Cross, has its own particular vibrational pattern.

7 "We have striven for simplicity of appearance in the Fundamental Symbols as an aid to memory while in use during meditation periods. Simplicity is the key to the subconscious mind. These symbols are designed to awaken the soul by triggering a particular inner spiritual response. Each basic component follows a sequence that projects its thought in unity of Reaction upon the viewer."

3 "We invite you to meditate using the Universal Law Symbols, to realize that their principles are expressed in actions, as manifestations of the Infinite Being--in all Creation, but particularly in your life. As this is done, going from one symbol for each Law to another, it will give you more *insight* into the

significance of the Master Symbol as a whole!"

The meditative process that is used for becoming aware of the Source and the Laws of the Universe within, consists of four simple steps. Four diagrams have been drawn, one above each step, to illustrate the meditative Slide of Awareness. The concept is to "slide" the focal point of your mental awareness between the conscious and subconscious mind (areas of awareness), depending upon whether you are *sending* or *receiving* a response. A dot will appear on a line within a circle, which can move in either the conscious mind (C), or the subconscious (SC) direction from the center of the subliminal mind (S).

1. RELAX

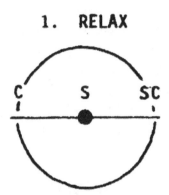

Relaxation is needed first of all to enter the subliminal state. Therefore, relax by holding a mental picture of the line with the dot at the center of it. Still the active, or conscious, mind. Think of nothing. Make a complete circuit of the nervous system with all stimulus (audio-visual). Allow it to move along the spinal column, up to the center of the emotional feelings (thalamus), then through it and up to the center of the discriminating thoughts (cortex), then through it. Then allow all stimulus to move back down through the thalamus and into the nervous system. Maintain a conscious awareness of this stimulus moving up to and down through the cortex.

When both centers are in an integrated and balanced relationship, they will produce unlimited subtle differences in the flow of thoughts and feelings.

2.   SEND

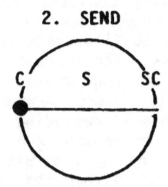

Next, in order to send or project a desire to awaken (develop synaptic connections between cortex and subcortex, or white matter) the larger eighty-two percent of the brain, mentally move the dot toward C position, to allow the conscious mind to think on the Master Symbol pattern. As soon as you have formed (visualized) the thought, slide the dot back to the center promptly to position S. In other words, picture the Master Symbol and go within to the Source.

3.   RECEIVE

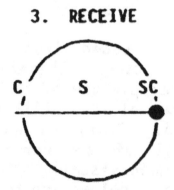

Now, from position S, mentally move to position SC, and you are ready to receive a response from your inner mind. Become aware of the real permanent intelligence and power within you. This includes the knowledge of many experiences you have accumulated until now, from previous

incarnations. Consider each oart, or memory
in detail.

Then, develop an individual awareness of
each part, as it is associated to each Law
Symbol, encountered in the All Mind. Do not
depend on previous impressions, or those of
others. Allow a composite pattern to form,
so that some purpose to life will unfold from
within. As a consequence, subconscious
thoughts can be updated, so to speak. Seek
to understand all portions of your awareness
of the Original Creation (Reality), and your
unseen spirit, or eternal consciousness within
it.

4. REALIGNMENT

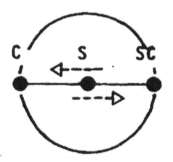

Now, mentally move the dot from position
SC through S, to C, and back again, in 12
gradual (slow) alternating motions, as vibrations between two tuning forks, in *resonance*.
4 "Realignment of the soul can occur when you
open your eyes and gaze steadily (in a relaxed
alpha state) at the individual Law Symbol,
then close your eyes. Allow this symbol to
come toward you, to be visualized, and rest
within the eighty-two percent area (white
matter) of the brain. It will appear to become luminous. As it does so, hold the symbol within the active eighteen percent area of
the brain, allowing the Light (Intelligence)
to flow into and envelope your creative
thought image (symbol). This will serve to

release tension and remove barriers, so that
you can enter the higher inner centers of the
psyche.

"Then reverse the process, and allow the
individual Law Symbol to return to the paper
before you. You may then pause quietly, to
become aware of any response that flows through
the greater area of the brain from the All
Mind." After a period of some 10 to 20 minutes, then relax and return to normal conscious
(cortical) brain activity.

"You may meditate upon each individual Law
Symbol once every 24 hours, or you may move
quickly from one to another in sequence, using
all 12 Law Symbols for a longer period of
meditation.

"Certain Law Symbols will have more results
with you than others, depending upon your
Inner Awareness and previous experiences of
life. All of these Law Symbols should be allowed equal meditation time, to release an
awareness of your inner level of being. When
you have completed the process with each Law
Symbol, experiencing specific responses of
remembering, then you may advance to meditation
upon the entire Composite Law Symbol as one
complete unit.

"In meditating upon the Master Symbol, re-
peat steps 1 through 4, as you would with each
component Law Symbol. Gaze upon it while in a
relaxed alpha state, for a period of 15 to 30
minutes; then close your eyes and draw the
entire Master Symbol into the inner area of
the brain. Hold the image there until you are
ready to release it back to the drawing that
is before you. It is at this point in your
meditative advancement that a greater response
on the ultraconscious level of Mind will come
to you."

When this meditation exercise is practiced daily, and especially before retiring, you will be capable of remembering all the knowledge and wisdom that the body absorbs during the hours of sleep. This method of meditation, together with a piece of Quartz, Amethyst, Lapis Lazuli, or Boron Crystal, on a band, placed over the center of the forehead, should greatly assist you in your understanding of the Master Symbol, its purpose, and enable you, with devotion and practice, to succeed in your purpose. Meditation and concentration will bring you awareness.

*   *   *

3. AWARENESS

Awareness is the link to the inner being and to the Creator. It is an inner knowing.

All, since their creation as conscious beings, were given the ability of awareness, to understand the Creative Spirit within themselves. *Awareness* is of the Mind, that is part of the soul, memory. Consciousness is of the physical brain, with its active thought. When perception of self is in relationship with everything, the awareness of being is complete. The immortal spirit or higher self is integrated when the primary principles of Life (Power), Light (Intelligence), and Love (Creation), are blended together in the *conscious mind.*

Our ability to sense the qualities of the Creative Consciousness as expressions of Life is the direct confirmation that these properties exist within ourselves. Otherwise, we could not respond to their attributes. It is only by mutual resonance that we experience. To be constantly aware of the original reality of Creation is to be aware of the principles of nature constantly in operation, and of all that there is. Any individual can instruct himself to permit this awareness to express through his form and blend with his Creator, as one.

The evolution of thought on this planet has brought about a state of hypnosis, which tends to separation from a complete awareness. It is difficult for us to look about and realize, or recognize, truth. We have been so conditioned, through the thoughts of others, to see things as they are given to us rather than as they really are, which is, simple. To be truly free, we must maintain a constant awareness of our spiritual nature and divine purpose. To achieve this, considerable effort must be applied through self discipline.

It is essential to be aware of our true position in Creation, and then to act in a manner that is consistent with that awareness. The more aware we become, the more we are capable of understanding the truth of our own soul and our reason for coming to Earth. Understanding is unitary, or oneness. Realization is all that separates people. We are here for two basic purposes:

a. To advance our personal vibration or character of thought, by experiencing the struggle between inner spirit and outer body, on a plane of greater density.

b. To awaken the dormant memory of our *Mission of Service, to assist the people of Earth to increase their awareness of reality.*

We must inevitably manifest the Creator fully. Any erroneous thoughts which interfere with this return to unity must be refused. It is the image *within* ourselves that determines the *outer* image. Gradual awareness and grasping of concepts of higher Truth come with evolvement of the soul, mind and body. These are ever striving upward toward perfection and oneness with the Source. Truth will be revealed to our awareness only in a state of perfect unity.

Awareness is automatic knowledge of the basic components of life and the Laws of the Universe. It is an inner knowing, rather than an outer learning. Awareness concerns the inner meaning and workings of the flow of life.

It is in part a sensitivity to the proper course
of Life. Awareness is of All Mind within the
Multiverse. It permits us to look down a long
series of incarnations, to reevaluate the course
of our purpose. Our awareness is oriented to
eventually return to the Source from whence we
came, as perfected beings. We are on Earth,
for the most part, to develop our awareness.
Intuition is one aspect of awareness.

We are given the ordained opportunity of
experiencing all parts of Creation in all
twelve dimensions, throughout eons of time
and places in the Cosmos. We are given the
right to become aware of every combination of
form and substance throughout all stages of
development, according to our own free will
choice. Our freedom is to express Spirit,
which is eternal in itself. Each expression
varies from every other, and the individual
background of experience serves as a foundation for the fulfilling of a particular destiny.

When we become aware of Life in its infinite
sense, by matching our conscious mind with the
original thought pattern of Creation, it produces an inner frequency in Harmony with it.
There are few barriers to our consciousness,
when in this state of unity. Love is total
unity, or understanding. When the memory block
is removed, no further assistance in this area
is needed from others, and we can then com-
mence our task.

In order to gain true Life, we must lose
the aspect of self, which is only for self,
and become aware of our personal identity in
service to all Creation. When we pledge ourselves to serve with others for the mutual
benefit of all, and prove it, the mission will
appear. And, when we are aware of things which

the majority of people ignore, inevitably we
will be contacted and prepared for events
yet to come.

We must attain a certain level of awareness
of spiritual, mental, and moral enlightenment
in order to be evacuated, and later repopulate
Earth. When we have achieved basic knowledge
to obtain a transformation of our molecular
structure and to elevate the vibratory pattern,
then we will be ready for dwelling on a higher
dimension. The nervous system, brain, and muscles of matter vibrate within certain limits,
and cannot increase or decrease greatly without some form of malfunction occurring. The
difficulty of coordinating the Spirit and the
Body may also require artificial adjustment of
the Life Force and frequency which form the
relationship or pattern of complete being.

As we progress, one step at a time, in our
comprehension of the Universal Laws, we eventually become aware that our purpose in life
is to grow. The more we are elevated by our
application of them, the more we are gifted
with the ability to assist others to grow also,
through Service.

*   *   *

4. SERVICE

Service is the way that Creation operates. It is cooperation, making growth possible.

Service is the natural way of the Creator. It is the plan of Creation, in which all is performing a service. Life itself in every manifested form is the result of the simplicity and totality of the Plan of Service. All things are interrelated parts and must cooperate with each individual segment of the whole, which brings forth the highest attributes in all. All parts of Creation act to support all other parts.

The original concept of mutual service, understanding, and love generated the entire integral universe. The desire to serve is *within* every part that exists. *Only through service may one be served.* In serving others, through assisting them to fulfill their desire to progress, we serve ourselves by aiding ourselves in fulfilling our desire. Through the experience of service, we build an indepth and complete understanding of the plan of Creation, which is the purpose for physical life.

Service has two primary objectives:

a. Transient or unlasting services performed on a daily basis for others.

b. Permanent or everlasting services performed to contribute toward the spiritual evolvement of others, by providing them with the influence and information necessary for its attainment.

Seeking understanding through service brings evolvement. When we recognize that we grow

through selfless service, and balance our
spiritual debts, we consider it an opportunity
to enthusiastically remove any barriers toward
achieving complete awareness. Service is an
unfoldment of accepting and understanding the
presence of the Creator within all others.
The goal is to attain Cosmic Consciousness.
It is only possible to attain this state
within, and demonstrate it through our interaction with our fellow beings. Within us is
the Creative Thought that generated All and
provided that all interact in a manner that
returns support to All That IS.

The planet Earth is currently in a state of
transition toward a greater unfoldment of progression. Through service, our world is of-
fered the means of establishing an Era of Enlightenment on Earth. People were reborn from
other planets and dimensions and placed upon
the planet, receiving assistance, contacted,
and awakened, in order to disseminate certain
facts concerning the Universal Laws of Evolutionary Progress. These volunteers were born
with an awareness of truth within themselves,
and have the ability to handle ridicule or
attacks upon that truth.

There is a cosmic order of beings who are
united for the cause of enlightenment throughout the inhabited planets of the Multiverse.
Specific primary units of men and women have
either incarnated, or been preconditioned to
live here, who have come from other planets
and dimensions to complete a task that they
know how to fulfill. Each moderates another
when too little is accomplished or when certain limits are exceeded. No person upon this
planet will know them, except those to whom
they reveal themselves, for a purpose, but not
to all.

We are being observed by people representing many galactic systems, and they are making
contacts with a few necessary service personnel on Earth in an effort to assist us toward
attaining a higher understanding of Life. We
are all citizens of the Cosmos, and not of just
one planet. They have come with the purpose
of alerting us to the coming changes in our
solar system, which will be numerous.

Consider, then, that this great work of enlightenment and preservation is being carried
on by a universal group of men and women with
contacts in every government of the world
and in every walk of life. This group is dedicated to saving the human race and preserving
the planet Earth, so that we, too, can enter
the Integral Universe, traveling to worlds
throughout. They desire to help expand individual perception. One can live above Cause
and Effect through a higher awareness of Universal Laws.

When anyone is to receive assistance from
any source, he must first accept completely,
both the assistance and the source. One individual must not force another individual to do
anything (even accepting his own God-self)
against his will. When advanced concepts and
methods are superimposed too quickly on less
advanced ones, the results are sometimes disastrous.

People exist in other than the physical
plane or density than our senses perceive.
the term "plane" refers to a high or low frequency level on which both spiritual and material beings can and do reside. Some of them
seem to be half etheric and, at times, are
invisible. The upper levels (fifth and beyond)
are known as *Etheria*, a place of high vibrational density as compared to our plane. Many

act and look just as we do, when one is able
to see clairvoyantly into these other dimensions, which begin between the infrared and
ultraviolet portion of the electromagnetic
spectrum. Above these levels, and extending
to infinity, are zones inhabited by those who
have advanced to the point of pure mental or
spiritual essence. Those who have attained
these levels never return to any material level
to reincarnate, except on rare periods of temporary descent to convey information to those
on that plane.

The means of identification which the people from other worlds and dimensions use would
mean nothing to most of us, as they are syllabic sounds that are direct conversions of
pictographic symbols, or purpose concepts.
These are conveyed through telepathic communications as a thought language. We have attempted to give, instead, those terms or names
which would be understandable when translated
into our written language. In actuality, only
the essence of any being or group defines their
purpose.

The Guardians are incorporeal beings, and
partially unmanifest. They exist and function outside of any physical dimension of the
Multiverse structure, in the uppermost regions
on a totally non-physical plane. The Guardians
are immortals who in consciousness dwell in
'soul essence,' inaccessible to physical realms,
from which they oversee the proper functioning and evolving of our physical worlds, making minor course changes that are in accord
with the overall Divine Plan, when necessary.

*The Interdimensional Federation of Free
Worlds* comprises 24.5 galactic systems, covering 33 vast sectors of space in a large disc
unit. This Intergalactic Confederation is

actually an all-encompassing body. The Federation (for short) Conclave of 5,000 Elder Masters from the quadrants of each galaxy meet once in every 450 years at the central nucleus of this intergalactic system located in the constellation of Virgo. The Federation is a loosely knit commonwealth of thousands of star systems in the multidimensional Cosmos.

The Galactic Confederation comprises 51 solar systems operating in over one sector of the Universe (or Federation). It consists of a network of beings originating from many planets (608) and dimensions, which vary from one another in progression. This includes some 3.5 million designated spacecraft. The purpose of the Galactic Confederation is to assist any solar system to achieve its scheduled development.

The Interplanetary Confederation comprises 10 (out of 12) planets within our star (Sol) system. It consists of an overall Spiritual Hierarchy, known as 'The Brotherhood of Light,' under the guidance of Elder Master Jesus-Sananda. The Confederation of Planets has a fleet of about 5,756 spacecraft and a comparable amount of service personnel, under the command of Ashtar Gabriel (or Sheran). The Galactic Confederation has volunteered some 1.05 million (30 percent) of its fleet, on standby, under the temporary control of Ashtar, in the event of possible evacuations.

The Planetary Coordinated Network comprises some 4 independent global area directors, 12 co-directors (assistants), 32 unit or base commanders, 96 field observation coordinators, and undeterminable amount of field agents. The Network (for short) consists of representation from the Guardians, Federation, Confederation, and the Brotherhood of Light, which incorporate

the Ashtar Command. Every issue of importance
concerning security measures of planet Earth,
excluding possible evacuation plans, is con-
sulted upon and confirmed by the Interplanetary
Confederation. The Universal Laws prohibit
any interference from others unless interplanetary existence and development is threatened.

All Creation is one. Separation is an illusion. To act upon one part of the Multiverse is to act upon the whole. We are all a
part of the Integral Universe of Creation.
All is created equally, for us All. All is
available for us to use when we have the cooperation to share in its use. We limit ourselves only by our ignorance of the Plan of
the Cosmos.   Whoever is in need will be assisted, with none permitted to direct their
affairs, but only to assist.

G   "We are all citizens of the Universe. We
live in a tremendous solar system and have an
Interplanetary Confederation guarding its affairs. Besides the Interplanetary Confederation, our solar system is within a galactic
system or Galactic Confederation. Beyond that,
all of the galactic systems and solar systems
are within the intergalactic system or the
Interdimensional Federation of Free Worlds.
In the Cosmic Scheme of things, all are interrelated, side by side allies, like a group of
good neighbors.

"Because our solar system happens to be one
of many in the galactic system, the association of solar systems, or Galactic Confederation, is willing to assist our individual
solar system with our problems. But they cannot issue directives to that individual solar
system, regardless of the circumstances. The
solar system decides whatever is best for
their own system. The Galactic Confederation

may advise or suggest, but they cannot en-
force. There is a guideline agreement on procedures, but basically they act independently
within their discretion. There is a give-and-
take, within some overlapping areas."

It appears that the present civilization, or
nations of our world, will not accept such assistance, reasoning that it would disrupt the
individual governmental, economic, and social
structures. Our civilization has that inalien-
able right of choice, which inevitably unfolds
the related consequences of that choice.

Our friends of many planets and dimensions
have been highly active in encouraging and precipitating their four steps of the Great Awakening for the past four decades. Their wil-
lingness to share, combined with humanity's desire to receive, merges to become spiritual
growth and development for the planet and its
environment. We are among beings who serve all
of mankind in this planetary system and beyond.
They live for Peace, Love and Light.

An unselfish analysis made by the help of
others can be of benefit. For we can become
so involved with our problems on Earth that we
overlook some of the main points, while others
can see them. There are those who do exist,
who are qualified to guide through advice. No
correction is easily accepted by those being
corrected, but this must be faced by those
dealing with the masses, whether teacher or
assistant. This is the purpose of the Great
Awakening—to correct an oversight before the
problem gets beyond control.

★   ★   ★

SEVEN

THE GREAT LESSON

THE GREAT LESSON

The Evolution of Awareness is the primary objective of all life forms, regardless of the plane of existence they occupy. All equally learn by experience upon stages of evolvement, with one no greater than another. All have many lessons to be learned, that they may progress toward greater *unity of expression* with the Creator of All. Each individual has freedom to choose his pace. Evolution is a path leading us toward achieving the Fundamental Thought of Creation through oneness with the Infinite One.

Everything that exists in Creation is one Unit of Reality, which operates in perfect order, harmony, and balance through reaction to the Laws provided by our Creative Spirit. The Universal Laws are extensions of the Principle of Creation, which is the Force of Cause and Effect. Each of these Cosmic Principles, or Laws, are applicable on all planes of existence, as Creative Forces in action throughout the Integral Omniverse. Each planet and dimension of the Creator has its own characteristics, or special forces, that manifest and operate according to unchangeable laws. It is self evident that All Creation throughout the Infinite Whole is the direct or indirect manifestation of our Creative Spirit.

Karma is a condition of cause and effect, brought about by trial and error. Trial and error are only necessary in our evolution when we lack understanding of the Universal Laws by which everything is created, maintained, and developed. Karma is living with a *memory block* of an artificial condition which takes on reality only because we, in ignorance, agree that illusion should be so. Self Realization is an *awareness* of a natural condition. Experiences of trial and error teach us to be aware, or remember. When we set into motion a certain action through ignorance of the Law, we cannot be charged with the responsibility for its consequences. However, when we have learned the Law, and ignore it, then we are indeed accountable. *Once we learn through our own mistakes, we will return to oneness with the Source.*

In every situation of life there is a lesson to be extracted when we are *open* to its meaning. We are both the student and the teacher of our own life, by our own choices. When we ask for an experience and receive it, we must *apply* what we have received and *share* it. We must learn to apply knowledge once we have attained its understanding, or we will lose it. Life is a classroom, with those who assist us in our learning process. On Earth we have an opportunity to learn lessons in the origin and power of thoughts, emotions and physical expressions, with the effects that they can have on us, others, and our planet. Nowhere else in our solar system can such *experiences* of control be obtained!

We cannot progress without attaining an applied understanding of the Universal Laws, as Principles, to each stage of growth. Each rung we achieve on the ladder of life prepares us for learning on planets higher in evolution. Through *our own efforts* we evolve upon a higher plane. When one's awareness is exposed to conditions that bring about additional experiencing, it automatically causes an elevation in the degree of being conscious. That which was learned yesterday serves only as a stepping stone toward the greater truth we can learn tomorrow. The more we come to *know*, the more we will *understand*, and then our wisdom and common sense will increase. Once on the *right path*, it cannot be otherwise. We will remain subjected to this school of life, bound to the wheel of karmic retribution, until we learn this *Great Lesson*.

As we progress back to the Creator, we move through planes of life within gross and coarse physical forms, low in vibration, to etheric forms, high in vibration. The evolutionary level of our being must be adequate for a given world and dimension to move on up to it. Otherwise, we will constantly be required to return to live in circumstances which will allow us to learn our lessons and pass the necessary tests. In that process, we pay the debts that are pending in the cosmic levels of life, in the same manner they were self-created.

All major cosmic service is performed at the incarnate level. All our problems have to be surmounted and overcome here on Earth. The penalty of failure increases each round, and our inability to overcome is more difficult. We must then *pause* to assimilate the lessons to be learned at *this* level. We came to this planet to learn, through many experiences, about the Laws that are a part of our inner being. We punish ourselves through actions that are in direct violation of these Natural Laws.

All of our past mistakes of trial and error

are summed up in this present age. Only through the serious consideration of history that has gone before can we hope to learn from our mistakes. The events that have taken place on our earth are statements of the operation of certain inescapable Natural Laws. An analysis of certain existing patterns and trends can be obtained that indicates the resulting occurrences were not necessarily inevitable. The sequence of experiences could have been changed had the activities been brought into balance with the Cosmic Principles.

We—each and every one of us—form a collective whole that is interdependent upon the sum of all our independent wills. We are responsible for ourselves, and for our input and output of thoughts and actions towards all others. Therefore, we can predetermine and alter what happens on the earth at this very moment. In our present world situation there are many people who are working within these Universal Laws to educate or influence their fellow man and woman, to change the course of action toward annihilation of the entire human race. However, there is no indication that it *will* be changed without working together toward a *United Awareness* of the Natural Laws of Evolutionary Progression. In so doing, we become aware of the struggle, through phases of development, that all life forms experience in order to grow.

No one can interfere with our will; another can only advise and instruct, when qualified to do so. The laws of our Creator give us freedom of choice of thought and action. They provide for harmony and purpose of all beings, on all levels of evolution, operating for their continual advancement to our Creative Spirit itself. We learn by the resulting experience of our will, which brings recognition of the

Laws of Nature that guide us through eternal progression to the Source.

The overall Cosmic Design unfolds in a gradual way, cycle by distinct cycle. For instance, our planetary cycles have led from crude primitive conditions toward more refined ones in every aspect. The cycle of change must always be reckoned with, whether geological or climatic; otherwise, we perish from the earth through our ignorance. We must learn to progress in rhythm with these natural changes and not be subject unto them. All cycles of experience are interlinked expressions of the Immutable Laws of Growth and Development. Both cycles and laws govern every aspect of our lives.

There is, throughout the Cosmos, an "Ascending Scale of Progress," consisting of many vibration levels interpenetrating one another. These dimensions manifest on levels that exist within the limits of their range of stationary vibration as to the density of matter. Outside of these limits, they are intangible. There are twelve levels of vibration in our galactic system, or sector of the Integral Universe we occupy. Each level is divided into twelve major and minor cycles. When a system of planets moves out of one density or dimension into another, it is known as a Master Cycle of Evolution, or a Cosmic Revolution, consisting of 28,791 (of our) years.

After we have *learned* the Great Lesson of the Master Cycle, we will be of value in our service to others. *We will have attained the vision of right choices.* With greater awareness concerning ourselves, we can gradually re-define our lives and express them in accordance with original purposes.

Learning results from releasing incorrect concepts and receiving truthful ones. Learning is change. Unlearning is difficult. Within each plane there are twelve lessons to be learned. Those that are interested in truth and advancement will learn and apply all of these lessons in accordance with the Universal Laws. As a result, they move up another rung on the ladder of life. Those who cannot change or progress must start over again. The cycle of evolution for the soul must be set back several millions of years, to *learn from the mistake of wrong choices.*

A pattern of actual history, which required 8.5 million years to unfold, will be presented as briefly and as accurately as is possible, so that we may *know* and *learn* from the experiences of the Great Lesson. This information is a composite of cross referenced facts obtained from the records of other planets in our galactic system of Vela. Recurring, or cyclic, events were used as the means to calculate time periods that form the basic sequence of connecting links and place every detail into a proper viewpoint within the whole.

*   *   *

The Origin of Man

D6   "Within the Universe of galactic systems there have always existed many types of creative evolution. Basically, they all came from the same lifestream. Man, being the highest in perfection within this lifestream, is similar in physical appearance wherever he is found." Man was created through millions of solar systems, and did not evolve from the lower animals. There were systems of planets without number, inhabited by a race of cosmic

beings in the form of Man, billions of years
before our solar system was even in the forming stage. Then, as now, there was interplanetary travel within and between systems, to
study the activities of space and of its
phases of development.

Within our galactic system of Vela, the
race of Man originated from the solar systems
in the Pleiades, and Orion, located near its
nucleus. Over many millions of years they migrated throughout the galaxy and other dimensional realms. The appearance of Man in physical form is but one of many manifestations
along the path of progress.

The Creation of a Solar System

A system of planets, like any other form,
requires a certain period of time to complete
a cycle of formation, development, and disintegration, to return back into its original
state of cosmic substance. Our solar system
was created about 1.5 billion years ago in magnetic balance, consisting of twelve planets
and one sun. It takes five to fifty million
years for each planet within the system to attain its full growth, depending on its mass.
It requires another five to thirty million
years before it is in a state ready for habitation.

The Survey of a Planet

When a planet within a system was found to
be in the process of formation, it was closely
observed by a survey team of selected scien-
tists in an orbiting laboratory craft. When
it became capable of supporting the race of
Man, the patrol informed the Galactic Council,

on the planet Terminus Hatonn, in the Andromeda system.

The Formation of Earth

D6   "Before our planet began to form, there was a huge (neutral) area of space. This dark void was an area that those of all planets were forbidden to enter. Our Divine Creator was gradually creating a new planet, known as Terra. The dark area required two million years to gradually lose its darkness. During the three million following years many changes took place upon this new planet. For over one and a half million years it glowed with a brightness which was beautiful. Ultimately it transformed into the appearance of a planet, ready for various forms of life." Earth was the third and slowest planet to reach this stage of development. Approximately 2.2 million years ago, Terra was found suitable for colonization.

The Councils on Settlement

Seven million years after Earth began to form, councils met on Venus, Terminus Hatonn, and other worlds, concerning the immediate intended purpose of settlement. Qualified volunteers (couples) were sought who desired to come to this planet for developing it. Nearly one million people from the Vela system elected to colonize Terra. Later, those from many of the other solar groups of the Galactic Confederation of 690 planets joined the program.

The Colonization of Terra

A race of parapsychic beings known as *Man* was placed upon Earth from other planetary systems, soon following. Animal life was also

brought here. However, plant life is a natural evolvement of our planet. Most of the
original colonists came from a star galaxy on
the right hand side of our Milky Way. Cargo
carrier craft brought these pioneers to the
new world with all essentials, including special equipment to record all events. Following occupation, frequent return visits were
made to bring additional supplies and equipment to these transplanted people, to establish the first civilization. This culture's
history is not recorded.

D6   "About seven hundred years of progress followed before most of the people from Venus returned, telling of unheard-of beauty and scen-
ery, and a true paradise. Those who remained
here worked with the forces of nature and
speeded up the evolutionary cycle of certain
animal species, while destroying the gigantic
mammals and amphibians that threatened man's
habitation."

     The planet Earth was colonized many times
by races from other solar systems. Twenty-
four civilizations of very great achievement
arrived, settled, and departed over the course
of 690,984 years.

The Civilization of Triteria

A   "The Triterian civilization, as those before
it, did not experience the destruction as those
who would follow. We have one symbol on Earth
today of this culture, in a deity called "Tri-
ton." He was worshipped by the Dogon tribe,
who picture the deity as half man and half
fish, symbolizing mastery over all elements of
nature." The actual symbol used to identify
these colonists that came from the Sirius

system 1.5 million years ago was a triangle en-
closing a circle with a dot in the center ⟁.

They remained until disaster occurred which
resulted in the destruction of their cities and
work. The perpetual cloud formation or mist
surrounding the planet, which acted as a protective filter system to weaken the destructive
rays of the sun, began to dissipate. The mois-
ture contained in these clouds fell as rain,
precipitating flood conditions. They returned
to the mother ships and orbited Terra. Water
destroyed everything. Beyond the flood they
came back down once again to the land surface,
deciding that instead of colonizing in one
area and risking recurrent destruction, they
would depart to different areas of the world
and settle underground.

The people of Triteria realized that conditions on the surface would not be favorable for
life within two hundred years. They built
twelve primary observation bases, rather than
cities, at major transit vortices of the globe.
Some ten thousand small discs used for monitor-
ing the environment of a planet, or space,
were converted to relay beacons, and adjusted
to land 500 miles apart from each other at
minor magnetic nodes. When this project was
completed, the grid power system became op-
erable.

As the cloud cover gradually dissipated,
the stars became visible through the atmosphere for the first time. The deadly cosmic
rays beamed upon the planet, and the average
lifespan decreased very rapidly, from 1,000
to 175 years of age. The second generation
of Triterian offspring, though born underground,
to the amazement of everyone, had no complete
recall of their prior lives and had to be

educated. The parents, with complete recall, realized their lack of recall was caused by an environmental situation.

H15   "According to survey records of early space probes passing near to the sun's corona, a condition of inhibiting radiation had existed for about 1.5 billion years. It was then determined that the element of gas known as Xenon, which is capable of shielding the harmful biological effects of the solar Lambda radiation, must be present in adequate amounts in the ionosphere. It was discovered to be in insufficient quantity, thus producing memory blocks in the brain as part of an overall genetic mutation."

"Nine months of exposure were required before effects appeared, creating conditions of combativeness, which was common to all life forms upon the surface." Because of these factors they decided to leave Terra. As a result, all inhabitants with but a few exceptions packed essential items into shuttle craft and cargo compartments of the mother ships. This race then transported itself from Earth to other planets. The few that chose to remain suffered from gradual mental and physical deterioration over a period of several generations, an estimated 1.4 million years ago.

During the time of Triteria an age of grandeur prevailed, through cooperation and unity of purpose, for the benefit of all the culture. Their civilization was built upon Universal Science, developed from the knowledge of the Master Symbol of Creation. It comprised a composite system of twelve Laws of Evolutionary Progression, consisting of the Cosmic Plan for equal development of the Spiritual, Social, and Material phases of life. This body of wisdom was obtained from the Source of All That IS, and preserved for the remnant.

Many geological changes took place upon this planet at that time, with earthquakes bringing about a new appearance to the contour of the land mass. The continent known as Triteria (Hyperborea) sank beneath the sea, and other new lands arose from beneath the waters. Once more, the earth was ready for further growth and development of life. Unfortunately, the harmful atmospheric conditions improved very little, and therefore, volunteers were not sought.

The Creation of Hu-Man

After these cataclysms, three hundred beings of the primitive race of Evas, an animal-like race, were brought to Earth from a planet in the Antares system 1.2 million years ago. These upright walking, intelligent creatures could reason things for themselves to a certain point. The Yeti, as they are now known, were brought to Terra to multiply and evolve. They survived well on this planet, but later the earth took another step forward, 1.18 million years ago. The Evas were also ready for advancement, and representative members of the Adamic, or Caucasian (white) race from the Orion system, came to propagate a new species. They chose to do this primarily through artificial insemination of Adamic genes (RNA/DNA) into female Evas, as a process of genetic mating. The results created mutant offspring that were neither completely true man or ani-man, as they were known then, and were given the name, "Hu-Man."

The Interference of Evolution

The Human and Evas race became resentful of

those from Orion performing these genetic experiments. Soon they bored tunnels throughout the body of Terra, and really began to revolt against the intruders. The genetobiologists left the planet, for they feared the creatures. Interfering with the normal evolution of Earth was not that which the Spiritual Tribunal of this solar system desired to do. The disturbance was curtailed. The planet was polarized, caused to turn on its axis, and in so doing create a magnetic vortex, to curtain it without an exit. The Evas, aware of these plans, disappeared inside the earth at a point in the Antarctic region, placing themselves in a state of suspended animation, to later come out from time to time.

Because the Human race inherited this primitive animal half nature, only about eight to ten percent were able to reach a spiritual state as pure Man had on neighboring planets. Many of those were unable to attain high evolvement, and did not survive.

The Civilization of Lemuria

The black race, or autochthonocus species, originated in a long evolutionary process, developing on the continent of Lemuria and into a civilization. Tribes of intelligent, simple, and humble Humans integrated together with their fellows (void of any parapsychic powers) and began building toward the future, founding the race of Lemuria. The great civilization of Lemuria existed until 60,000 years ago. Over a period of some 700,000 years the race gradually migrated to the coasts of South Africa.

The earth had two moons. The second was smaller in size and revolved in a larger orbit, about 1.8 times the distance of Luna. The planet's rotation and orbit around the sun was in a stable state, with two moons. The combined influence of both moons caused a marked increase in the size of man and animals.

The Destruction of Lemuria

The Cosmic Revolution, or Evolutionary Cycle of our galaxy, is 28,791 years. The planet *Hercolubus* revolves around its sun, known as Tila, twice each Evolutionary Cycle. Hercolubus is 266,625 miles in diameter, and requires 14,000 of our years to complete one orbit within the Tila system of planets. Thirty thousand years ago Hercolubus passed near the earth, violently attracting the smaller, more distant moon. The powerful influence of this massive planet changed Terra's axis of rotation, geography, climate, and ecology. When only Luna remained along with the earth, an unstable state was the result, causing it to wobble on its axis and become pear shaped and bottom heavy.

A series of cataclysms lasting 10,000 years caused much of the large continent of Lemuria to sink beneath the Pacific Ocean. During the flood and rebalancing of the earth on its present axis, portions of Lemuria were frozen quickly and swallowed under the ice in Antarctica. One of the names given to Lemuria (Mu) was, the Tree of Life. In this legend, the Tree was the civilization, and the Race was its fruit. Later, a great serpent (symbol for the waters) bit off (separated from the rest of the land) the Tree at its roots, and swallowed it (the culture).

From this Tree of Life have all the people

who now inhabit the earth originated. Scattered seeds, or remnants of mankind, were left here and there, from which other civilizations would, in time, develop. The remaining portions of Lemuria are known as Australia and New Zealand. The cataclysms began around the time of the last Cosmic Cycle, 28,774 years ago.

The Civilization of Atlantis

Venus was experiencing environmental changes during this period, which eventually would lead to the total extinction of life on that planet. The bronze, or red race, originated from Venus. Over a period of one hundred years, many of the inhabitants of Venus were transferred to Earth in different groups. The planet Lucifera assisted in this evacuation.

The civilization of Atlantis, with a central governing power on an extensive continent divided into ten provinces, was developed by these people ten thousand years later, or 18,774 years ago. During that time beings from other worlds chose to come to Earth to assist in the progression of its people. An elaborate complex of cities was built, both above and below the surface, linked by tunnels to many parts of the world. The subterranean network had a green luminescence which replaced the sun as a source of energy, and which made it possible for vegetation to be grown.

The Conflict on Lucifera

Among the planets, Lucifera (Lanka), meaning "Bringing Light," was the most radiant yellow planet in the galaxy. It was known as

Lucifera, after Lucifer, who became its last lord, and before that, as Filara. Lucifera revolved around the sun, known as Solas, between the orbits of Mars and Jupiter. This world had the least material density of any of the planets within the solar system. Its population was embodied then in the most attenuated manifestation of matter. The people of Lucifera were about 5 feet, 7 inches (1.72 meters) in average height, with racial characteristics (slightly conical heads) markedly different from ours.

On their native planet they knew only joy, health, development, unity and eternal life. The race of Man on Lucifera as a whole, preferred to live in peace and harmony with all Creation, although there were some who had grown in personal ego and aggressiveness. These individuals, through greed, desired to assume power over the others. Despite the teaching, which indicated the *absolute necessity of Man's expression conforming to the Universal Laws*, some developed, instead, attitudes which led toward evil. In the glory and wonder of their world they grew proud and arrogant, until there was a conflict among the people.

There followed a period of war and temporary peace between the two major governments on Lucifera. Those who could not be assimilated into its two major cultures, because of an inferior moral level, were brought to Earth 14,600 years ago. They were situated in the fertile but uninhabited territories of what is now known as the Middle East. Another group was transported later to the Black Sea region between the Dnieper and Danube Rivers. These then migrated north and into all of Europe.

A coming Cosmic Catastrophe was predetermined twenty-two years later, that would destroy Lucifera in two-hundred years. It was foreseen and calculated that a thermonuclear explosion would occur, triggered by many factors, including the passage of a large planet. Everything was done to warn and assist the people before this impending cataclysm took place. A portion of one-third of the population of one empire, known as Munt, responded to the warning. It was decided that the nearby moon of Jupiter, known as Ganymede, would be prepared for habitation within ninety years. Upon completion, those that chose to leave were evacuated in stages over a period of one hundred years. Most elected to settle in the underground environment of Ganymede, which had a controlled environment. Other individuals went to Atlantis, on Earth.

Approximately 14,378 years ago, as predicted, tremendous geological disturbance, such as quakes and volcanic eruptions, took place all over Lucifera. There was confusion, panic, and terror amongst the people on the surface. A nuclear war broke out on Luficera, as a result of ignorance and the problem in getting along with one another, turning ultimately against the Great Giver of Life. Within a few days, a Hydrogen Bomb was detonated, and the entire planet gradually became as bright as a sun, while converting itself into a supernova. As a consequence, Lucifera's binding vortex was disrupted, and the planet exploded, reducing it to oblivion. Lucifera became an asteroid belt, throwing its debris outward in all directions, as well as destroying its two moons, known as Lillith and Malona.

The Destruction of Atlantis

Earth was in a different cosmic position at that point in time. After a collision of planets, it was motionless for one revolution. Tidal waves rocked the planet, while enormous volcanic fires burned. A tertiary moon known as Azlan, or Bal, came in contact with Earth's upper atmosphere and was torn to pieces by conflicting forces. These fragments fell upon Terra as meteors, with a few of them remaining in orbit as a ring of debris. During this great cataclysm the continent of Atlantis sank beneath what is known as the Atlantic Ocean.

The planet Earth was then hurled from its rightful place and burned from friction. Both Earth and Mars were catapulted into new orbits. The resulting disturbance also changed the position of the primary moon, Luna, making conditions for surface life extremely difficult. After being thrown off course, Terra settled into a new wider orbit. The surviving remnant discovered 365 days in a year, instead of the previous 360 days. While our planet was re-orienting its axis, Mars' oceans were being ejected into space, and later caused a Great Flood upon Earth. Within three months over two-thirds of all humanity on Terra were the fatal victims of this devastation.

The Disaster on Mars

There were overwhelming disasters of all kinds on Mars, including volcanic eruptions, and many of its people perished. Two artificial satellites, known as Phobos and Deimos, had to be quickly constructed and placed in two different orbits to readjust Mars' unstable condition, and to prevent the planet from being thrown out of the solar system.

The Pole Shift of Earth

The remaining survivors on Earth endured the process of a thirty degree polar tilt and a magnetic reversal of the planet, occurring within a span of one hundred and two years, 13,600 years ago. This shift of geomagnetic poles, with a gradual drop in protective field intensity to zero level, resulted in exposing all life forms to intense cosmic radiation, which later created genetic mutations. Mankind, as a result, gradually reverted back to the Stone Age type of being. The change of polarity also produced an Ice Age upon the planet. The earth, being further removed from the source of solar heat chemistry, became considerably colder as the Glacial Period began nearly 13,000 years ago and lasted for 1,500 years. Earth received a more intense destructive blast from Lucifera than did Mars, and has not yet fully recovered from this event.

The Rise and Downfall of Planets

It was due to Man's misunderstanding of atoms that this became the war to end all wars, as well as everything else on Lucifera. It should be well remembered that fission and fusion of elements is an activity that belongs on suns, not on planets. When negative elements that make up the planet are forced into positive reaction, these elements then act in opposition to everything on the negative planet, producing a destructive effect. The planet then becomes out of balance, life supporting force is diminished, and, if allowed to take on overpowering control of its negative nature, it will explode into cosmic debris. When the planet Lucifera had *fallen*, destroying itself, the only remaining evidence of its once great civilization was the radioactive asteroid belt. This sterile and barren ring of meteors is a non-harmonious and non-balancing influence for our solar system. There are other shameful cosmic displays of this type which insult the Creator of the Universe. This should serve as a "Great Lesson" and warning to all those who know of the rise and downfall of planets.

The Intergalactic Conclave

The First Intergalactic Council of Elder Masters was held 650 years ago, or in 1334, resulting in the Formation Assembly which, in turn, effected the unison of a great number of inhabited worlds into the tremendous organization known as the Interdimensional Federation of Free Worlds, All World Federation, and the United Galaxy Alliance of Worlds. According to Galactic Cycle, 28,124 years ago, 8.2 galaxies were represented by 417 solar tribunals, each comprised of twelve planetary Elder Masters. Another Intergalactic Council was held 28,324 years ago, or in 1534, concerning interference from another organization known as the Alliance of Righteous Worlds, Khorellians, and Legion, after which certain procedures were adopted and strategic actions taken.

The Development of Man

In the last few thousand years, through many ages, mankind has striven forward, from the Stone, Wheel, Iron, Steam, Electric, Flight Ages and into the Atomic Age. The last two ages have challenged man's mind to seek the mysteries of the Cosmos more than any other, but these will become the shortest lived, as he progresses. When a civilization has reached a specific level of inner seeking of the Truth of Creation, displaying the principles of Light

and Love to all others, then contacts occur
with those of other worlds.

Since 1913 Interplanetary Ships of the Galactic Confederation have orbited the earth
and have sent shuttle craft through its atmosphere. One of these carrier ships is known as
the Saturnia, with a well-trained crew from
the planets Venus, Mars, Jupiter and Saturn,
in our system. They serve in the Great Cause
to help us reach forward to a *New Level of
Awareness*.

The Atomic Experiment

In December of 1951, atomic experimentation
on our earth caused extreme volcanic eruption
on Mars. There was an unusual bright spot on
the Tithonius Lacus and a large "snow storm"
over the south polar region.

The New Cosmic Field

In 1952 this solar system entered into a
new cosmic field which has had and is having
a profound effect on this system of planets.
As our solar system progressed through space,
it crossed from density three to four on
August 20, 1953. In so emerging, everything
upon our planet must adapt to this higher frequency pattern (Blaau). All things in this
solar system are going to be brought into balance.

The Axial Tilt of Sun

This influence was greatly responsible for
the ninety degree axial turn of the sun on
October 24, 1959, changing from negative to

positive polarity. This magnetic field reversal took almost two years to complete, and is causing the interacting fields of space to make a similar change. Our planet, as a result of the polar tilt of the sun and our own geomagnetic field's attempting to remain the same, is causing a conflict between the two celestial bodies, creating geological pressures, earthquakes, and volcanic eruptions. Also, this has brought about a change in the global weather pattern, with the jet airstreams moving in new routes, as well as ocean currents, altering atmospheric pressures, and temperatures. It was time for a rebalancing of magnetic forces in the sun, so that all the planets could benefit and enjoy a type of cleansing and refining of magnetic forces in a new cycle of order.

The magnetic field strength of Terra began to slowly decrease between 1958 and 1959.

The Advantage of New Cycle

Nature is in a constant state of re-creation, or evolution, and never rests. We are also in this process of creation. That is the reason we feel that the perfection of ourselves is yet to come. But before this reality will become ours, we will go through many changes which will come much faster than those of the past—especially when we once begin to understand the Laws of Life under which we live, for at this very moment we are already beginning a new cycle of Life.

The Nuclear Disarmament

Many of the nations of Earth possess atomic and thermonuclear forces. An effective, total world disarmament will not be accomplished, due to lack of trust in the world between nations. A peaceful international fellowship cannot be established because we do not have the necessary high moral level which allows people to change their methods and structures of government without boundary lines.

It is imperative that use of free magnetic energy be brought about on our planet as soon as possible, if for no other reason than to take the place of atomic energy. Magnetic energy is far more safe in use. When this is realized, radioactive materials and atomic radiations can be neutralized and put aside. If man does not make the choice for progress, then he will digress and destroy himself as a result of the misuse of atomic power.

The Great Accident

The planet Terra is paralleling the conditions on Lucifera before it exploded. The causes for this were similar: greed, lust for power, envy, hate, and selfishness. The diabolical crisis—to dominate or have absolute power over the minds and wills of all beings, producing human robots—began through experiments to control the mind and consciousness of a few.

A Third World War could begin between the three major cultures, about 1986, as an inevitable outburst created by a few people, in the last general holocaust to affect our planet. This global conflict is being delayed until a Cosmic Cataclysm can intervene. If this does not occur, then it will be known as "The Great Accident." Wide devastation, suffering and death of many, will result from the holocaust of Armageddon, of the War of Desolation, which is not necessarily an absolute to come.

The Interdependence of Life

We are responsible for our part in the over-all progress or decline of living conditions, because of the basic interdependence of all life. A natural result of this sense of purpose will bring certain people together in a common awareness and mission of service.

The Interdimensional Federation of Planets, at the request of Galactic Confederation and the Solar Tribunal, has agreed to intercede to prevent total destruction of the planet Earth. It is hoped that by doing so, another, more Universal and Creative Civilization might take the place of the current destructive one. The spacecraft of many galactic systems have appeared with the purpose of awakening their own people, reborn on Earth from other planets. So it is, that they will awaken to the Laws, as they manifest in and through all Creation.

The Etherians are distant allies of the Interdimensional Space Federation, which includes the systems of Spectran, Psychea, and Omm Onn. The planet is being raised into another plane of higher vibration; therefore the potential for awareness increases. "Man is now at the point when he is awakening to the existence of his inherent rights, and will forge a new life for himself, in a New World." On September 1, 1975, the earth began to enter a more normal state of being. Everything on our planet began to receive positive rays which uplift and help mankind psychically, more than he yet realizes. It requires several thousand years before a biomagnetic change in people will occur. Certain people will be able to prepare or adapt, once they have been made aware of the impending disaster, but not many will consider the warning.

The Program of Assistance

All spiritual help possible will be given to everyone on Earth, from all parts of the Universe. The outcome of events on this planet depends entirely upon our progress in unity, understanding, and brotherly love during the time period left us between now and the year 1986. If we bring through too great a preponderance of evil here, it will mean another fall for us of Earth, into even denser meshes of materiality and unreality. It is an Immutable Law of the Cosmos, that too great a preponderance of evil inevitably results in self-destruction and a new beginning. This planet and some of its people will be saved, but in no time frame, or dimension, is the future ever written irrevocably.

Many geological catastrophes and impending major wars are kept deferred by minimal or covert means, in the hope of gaining time for a more peaceful transition to the New Cosmic Cycle, or Aquarian Age. So far, there is definitely hope for this to reasonably occur.

Beyond 1984 the Space Federation will no longer make major efforts to avert global disasters, but will, instead, shift the emphasis to immediate mass evacuation of those of the Forces of Light.

Humanity could fall because of its tremendous errors, by destructive influences, to be reborn out of its ashes later on, as the Phoenix was reborn.

The Operation Rescue

It is self evident that a more peaceful transition into the New Cycle would be more of a benefit for all concerned. The Space Federation has been trying to assist in improving conditions on Earth for a long time. In the event of the probable large scale devastations, it will have no other choice than to rescue as many willing people as is possible. The survivors capable of living in the stepped up vibration of the New Dimension will be a small portion of the total population. These higher types of individuals can be easily spotted through aura detection onboard designated shuttle craft and picked up by various methods.

Evacuation will not occur unless it is absolutely necessary, because a mass landing will have a gigantic psychological impact, thus affecting the destiny line of the human race on Earth, which should be worked out on its own. The Law is, that there is only progression and no regression. There are, at this time, only a few who can progress in the environment of this planet. All others will vanish in one way or another. The ones who chose not to live by the Universal Laws will be left behind for the impending catastrophe. The people who have chosen to live correctly, in accordance with the Laws, will be physically evacuated before the polar tilt, or disaster, happens.

In case of extreme conditions it will become necessary to actually ferry thousands of people at a time, by means of 'Space Arks', to large waiting mother ships. The people aboard these carriers will have come from many star systems, each doing his part in this enormous united operation to evacuate approximately ten percent of the population (400,000,000). The shuttle craft will come from large space stations in geosynchronous orbits, about one hundred miles above the earth. The space stations (bases) move according to an established and coordinated plan with one another. They are usually distributed in different places around our planetary system, instead of in fixed positions. The space arks used for transit between Earth and mother ships, or space stations, each has a full capacity for 2,500 men and women. Each space station has a capacity of 10,000 people.

When either the Third World War or a polar tilt commences, all those who have reached the highest level of evolution in humanity (indicated by a white aura) will have left the earth. They are going to be taken aloft where they can observe this planet change its upper strata layers, in a resurfacing action, as it has before, in previous civilizations. All those who have not been able to overcome the lower and middle levels of the astral plane will go to form part of the New Spiritual Population of the giant planet Hercolubus, in the Tila star system. They will be drawn to it by the vibratory attraction of that body. The evolutionary level of Hercolubus is comparable to prehistoric times on Earth. There they will develop at their own pace. It will be a hell to those who remember the higher standards of living on former Earth, to have to incarnate into and remain on this inferior savage world for many millions of years. But Hercolubus will be a fresh start for them in a new progression.

The Nova Terra Project

While inside the space stations, a vibratory shift will be made into a midway fourth dimension between Earth third and Etheria fifth. During this transition no actual distance has been traversed. The survivors of our planet will then be taken from the mother ships and transported to a planet known as *Nova Terra*. Others that volunteered for special assignments on Earth, and who are not a part of its evolutionary pattern, may be returned to their respective solar systems and dimensions of origin.

Nova Terra is a temporary shelter planet in a halfway dimension and orbit between the planet Earth and moon Luna. This planetoid is about 2,623 miles (4,220 km) in diameter, and 8,240 miles (13,258 km) in circumference. According to the population densities of Earth, one quarter of its surface could easily accommodate our present population of four billion without any undue cramping. It is large enough to tide over survivors, or the evacuated. Nova Terra is similar to the earth in environmental conditions, with facilities to accommodate great masses of people from our planet in the event of two possible massive disasters (thermonuclear war and magnetic polar shift).

The planet Nova Terra is presently populated by service personnel, consisting of those volunteers who set up things (construction technicians) and those who act as the translators, escorts and instructors. Ninety percent of these individuals are from all over the Federation, and ten percent are from Earth. When the survivors arrive on Nova Terra they will later be educated adequately and submitted to a long process of organic and physiological reconditioning which will permit them to live for several hundred years. In this way, they will be able to assimilate the enormous advancement of their instructors and prepare themselves to return to Earth, some time after 2001, to begin the New Age.

The end of an era is near; the only question is, when and how. The end (or new beginning) could come any time between 1984 and 1996, but by 1999 at the very latest. There is a catastrophe coming, either through one Final War or Nature. We have already discussed the potential for a Third World War, and now we will consider probable intervention from the Cosmos.

On December 14, 1984, a comet from the supernova Cassiopeia "A" will pass close to the earth. The planetary alignment which began to pull on the earth in 1982 will peak by the middle of 1985. In February, 1986, Halley's comet will also pass nearby. Every fifty-two years the Aztec calendar of 260 days (Venus year) and the agricultural one of 365 days (Earth year) start on the same day, usually meaning a minor change will occur. At fifty-two year intervals, meteorites come from the vicinity of the asteroid belt. The next time this will occur is in 1986. In March, 1987, a major change is expected to affect everyone upon Earth. The last time such an event took place was 450 years ago.

The asteroid belt, located between the orbits of Mars and Jupiter, is the remains of planet Lucifera. It consists of a wide trail of scattered sidereal bodies of every size, from simple cosmic dust (meteorites) up to masses (meteors) as large as the asteroid Ceres, whose diameter is almost 485 miles (780 km). When we account for the multiple sum of the orbits of all the planetoids that form this "ring," it is found to be about 155,380,000 miles (250 million km) wide.

In 1986, from the region of Vega, comes a comet that is 87,234 miles in diameter, which will pass through the asteroid belt and pull debris behind it. The comet will appear a red dot, then as a fiery tail of flame moving nearby the earth, and producing a meteor shower. A great stone will hit the planet as it passes through the tail of this comet. The currently proposed method, adopted by the military, for preventing comets or asteroids from striking the earth, is by using rockets equipped with *hydrogen warheads* to divert their oncoming path, or to alter their orbits.

Our sun appears to have a star orbiting it that passes by Earth once every 28 million years. It is known as "Nemesis," for it may produce storms of comets that periodically eliminate most of the life on our planet. A series of periodic catastrophic impacts on the surface of Earth is indicated geologically and by fossil remains. At this time, Nemesis was reported to be at the most distant point of its orbit around the sun.

A celestial body (giant comet, or planet) detected by satellite IRAS, which has a low temperature and emits or reflects no light, is apparently 45 billion miles away from Earth, according to NASA. Also, a new star was formed recently in the Taurus System.

Sometime between 1999 and 2001, the planet known as *Hercolubus*, which belongs to a planetary system of Tila, which is unknown to most people on this planet, will pass by us once again. Hercolubus passes within only 932,256 miles (1.5 million km) of Earth at its closest proximity. As a consequence its electromagnetic pull (pressure force) will reverse the magnetic poles of Earth, again change its axis of rotation, and in turn, cause the geographic poles to change position. This will bring about many upheavals, causing entire continents

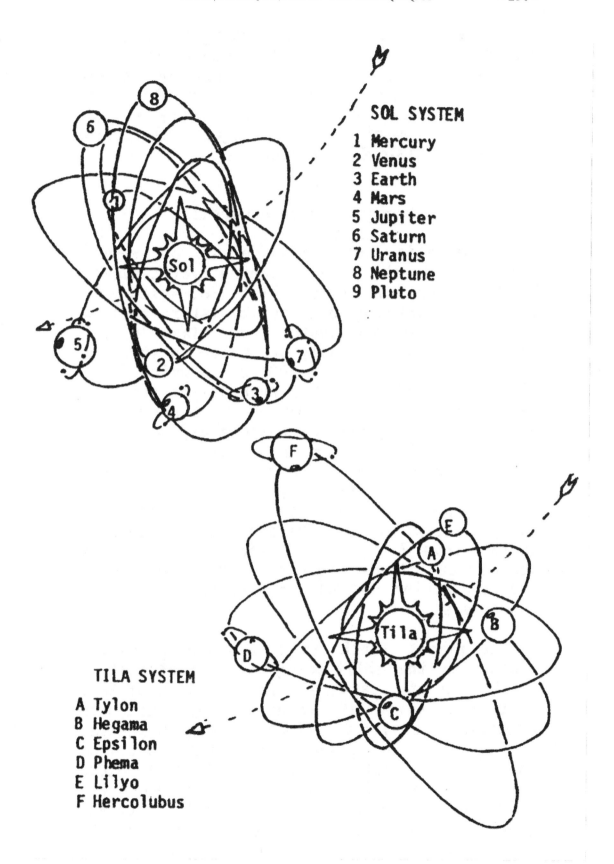

SOL SYSTEM

1 Mercury
2 Venus
3 Earth
4 Mars
5 Jupiter
6 Saturn
7 Uranus
8 Neptune
9 Pluto

TILA SYSTEM

A Tylon
B Hegama
C Epsilon
D Phema
E Lilyo
F Hercolubus

to rise and sink, thus transforming the planet.
Once the change is completed, another true Cosmic Revolution on an entirely new surface of
Terra will begin. This time a civilization
will end forever and will be replaced by another
culture of humanity, on a regenerated world
capable of Cosmic Consciousness.

The Magnetic Polar Reversal

The magnetic field collapse and polar reversal of Earth is a recurring cyclic event.
In 1993 a sun spot cycle will begin, which usually causes intense geomagnetic disturbances on
the planets of our system. Our planet's magnetic field has gradually decreased in strength
51 percent in the last 4,000 years, which indicates the beginning of a reversal of the magnetic poles. According to various archaeolo-
gists and geologists, magnetic field reversals
are estimated to occur a minimum of once in
every 450,000 years. During a reversal the
field oscillates, gradually drops in strength,
then disappears. A new field then emerges with
an opposite polarity. The process is calculated
to take from 2 to 20,000 years. During this
period ice clouds begin to form, triggered by
the penetration of solar radiation through the
ionosphere.

The planet Earth is in a state of evolution, with the shift being only a continuation
of its growth pattern. At the close of this
century a shift of the axis will occur, with
dramatic reversals of climate through a partial
rotation of the globe. The poles move from
one place to another once every 1,500 to 3,000
years. The actual polar shift itself will require about ninety days to reposition on new
poles. A drastic tilt of our earth would, to
some degree, affect all the other planets in

our galaxy, by change of its magnetic field relation lines of space.

Prior to the shift, warnings will be given through weather changes, with increase in heavy snowfall, strong gales, and humidity. There will also be geological changes as well, with moderate-to-intense surface tremors, or quakes, volcanic eruptions, and tidal waves. Then our planet will rock slowly, several days before it occurs. When it tilts on the side, stars, including our sun, will seem to stand still overhead, only to move backwards while the planet settles into its new orbit around the sun. Then the stars will be in the position of 15,000 years ago, some 22°, putting it back in its proper place, where Urticus may serve as the new Pole Star.

The magnetic grid system, with its stabilization generators (pyramids) will become activated and balanced between 1986 and 1996. The complete physical reversal of Earth's geographic poles will not occur because of the grid system of stabilization generators that maintain proper motion and magnetic field strength. When the planet passes through a certain threshold of imbalance, then the system is triggered to become active.

The Perimeter of Golden Light

In the Great Pyramid of Cheops in Egypt there is an ancient record of wisdom by those who planned it, that alludes to the star *Alcyone*, which belongs to the Pleiades (Taurus) system. Our entire solar system, including Earth by 2001 or beginning of New Cosmic Revolution of 28,791 years, will enter a zone of perpetual "Golden Light" which is located in part within the perimeter around the star

Alcyone.   It covers many light years distance
with a bright luminosity.   This is known as
the Realm of Cosmic or Christ Consciousness.

All of those who enter this realm have
reached the highest moral level which is possible on Earth. The aura light and color ra-
diance corresponding to the purest, highest
state of soul development in each of these
individuals is a mixture of bright white
light with tones of gold. Those who have already been "sealed," know their destinies into
the Cosmic Age.

The objective is for all people, including
the planet, to achieve oneness with the Creator. It has taken many stages of development
for this to be achieved. The earth is going
up one vibrational level, through an emergence
period, into a plane where the powers of Mind
operate in total harmony, as a new phase of
learning, if it survives. The dissolution of
time and space in a process of Mind must completely occur in order to enter a much higher
vibrational level, by the will of the Creator.

The Elder race has pointed out the way for
the Human race. In order to fulfill our proper
destiny in the Divine Scheme of Evolution, we
must control matter-energy-space-time, through
the subjective synthesis of telepathic inter-
play.

The Cosmic Age of Understanding

Once the Elect, or survivors on Nova Terra,
have adapted to this higher level of vibration,
after Earth's purification and magnetic balance
to the fourth dimension, they will be returned
to it for evolutionary reasons. "To them that
overcometh will I give to eat of the Tree of

Life, which is in the midst of paradise (Source) of God. Blessed are they that do His Laws, that they may have right to the Tree of Life (Eternal), and may enter in through the gates into the city (New Age)." Rev. 2:7, 22:14 There is a desire within our soul to reach the Infinite Source of All Knowledge and Wisdom of Universal Truth, within the Triune Godhead.

When the time comes for a New Culture, it will be based on equal development of every phase of life, in accordance with the Universal Laws. It will also be evident to all governments that Earth will have to be directed from one central government, and that no separate nation will direct. The only direction will be from the government that directs all the other planets in this system, and this governing body is located on Saturn. It has offices on each of the planets, but all are governed from the one central headquarters, which is known as the High Tribunal of the Great Confederation of the planets. The Solar Cross will be the only flag used on Earth, as it is now used on the other planets. This will mean all people under one flag, without divisions of creed, principles, or phases of life.

The Plan of the Creator is for the planet Earth's emergence into a Cosmic Age, when we have awakened to our place within the Universe. When this occurs we will then realize the complete scope and purpose of the Great Lesson, through *"The Master Symbol of the Solar Cross* $\oplus$ *."*

*   *   *

CONCLUSION

The Brotherhood (and Sisterhood) of Light provide only the necessary information to stimulate a Search for Truth. It is our responsibility to *assemble it* into *our reality*. We must maintain that objective to progress. It remains a matter of individual choice to progress, or to retrogress. It is our decision to choose to be creative or destructive. All species have their own individual places and privileges to exist in the Integral Multiverse and are permitted to fulfill their purposes.

The purpose of this task was to *assist you* in achieving awareness of our relationship to all life. Only by applying these lessons firmly, as your mind is prepared to receive them, will we depart this cataclysmic period, to return later. Rapid individual development will be necessary. Once these Essential Truths *are realized*, then we as interdependent and responsible members of this planet can cooperate towards progress as *One Civilization*. As a state of common sufficiency is acheived, progress in every phase of life becomes a reality.

This book is the creative resultant of a *cooperative effort* to assist one another. Therefore, any information that you feel is pertinent towards this composite point of view and service would be greatly appreciated as contributions. "The whole, is greater then the sum of its parts." "To everything there is a season, and a time to every purpose under the heaven."

In The Light of Our Radiant One, with Love,

Richard T. Woodmaster/ Tarvis

ACKNOWLEDGEMENTS

I wish to extend my humble and sincere appreciation to all those who have been either directly or indirectly instrumental in assisting me to bring you this composite message of hope and enlightenment. Through this COOPERATIVE EFFORT you, the Seeker of Basic Truth, can progress by its understanding and application. This is, in a sense, a Tree of Life, and Knowledge evolved through many experiences yielding fruit for all to partake of, and grow. Here are some of those who contributed to this book:

GEORGE ADAMSKI, who dedicated most of his life toward our acceptance, comprehension, and utilization of the Universal Laws, to bring about an Age of Cosmic Enlightenment.

MICHAEL X. BARTON, who, with Lonzara, shared many details with us concerning the Cosmic Principles pertaining to our evolutionary process.

JACQUES P. DRABIER, who, with Lattrob, channeled a variety of information on such subjects as the Symbols of Reality and the Frequency Barrier.

CALVIN C. GIRVIN, who, with his contact, Cryxton, made references to several events which occurred during the early colonization of Earth.

WILLIAM GRAY, who, by tuning in on the Ring of Power encircling the earth, was able to learn about, use, and instruct others in the use of Magnetic Life Rays.

GABRIEL GREEN (Editor), who, with Robert P. Renaud, in contact with the Universal Alliance of Planets, is dedicated to assisting us in our collective efforts toward progress.

RICHARD T. MILLER, who, with the cooperation of many others, both on earth and other worlds, aided us with much information and techniques to develop an awareness of Life throughout the Universe.

JOHN REEVES, who had received a message written in a language known only to a few on Earth, concerning the detrimental effects of nuclear radiation (tests) on the planets of this star system.

TUELLA, who, with the Great Brotherhood of Light, is dedicated to channeling information that is vital to our spiritual growth and awakening.

PARTANA VEGAN, who, with Akasan, has provided us with many answers concerning our unfoldment, in accordance with the Evolutionary Plan of Creation.

GEORGE HUNT WILLIAMSON, who is a pioneer in the areas of Anthropology, Etymology, and Archaeology, has written several books dedicated to the service of enlightening those wanderers on the path of growth and development through service to all.

These individuals are but a few of the many who make up the Universal Network of World Servers, known as the Great Brotherhood (and Sisterhood) of Light overseeing the Evolutionary Plan for All on planet Earth.

Richard T. Woodmaster/
Tarvis

BIBLIOGRAPHY

A. George Adamski*, 1961, 'Flying Saucer Fare-well,' Abelard-Shuman Limited.

B. Michael X. Barton*, 1967, 'The Venusian Secret Science,' Futura Press, CA.

C. Jacques P. Drabier, 1967, 'Prism Newsletter,' M.I.N.D., Hollywood, CA.

D. Calvin C. Girvin, 1958, 'The Night has a Thousand Saucers,' Understanding Publishing Co.

E. William Gray*, 1952, 'Know Your Magnetic Field,' Life Energies Research, CA.

F. Gabriel Green, 1963, 'UFO International,' Issue 19, Amalgamated Flying Saucer Club of America, Inc., P. O. Box 39, Yucca Valley, CA 92284.

G. Oscar Magocsi, 08-1984, 'Luminarians,' Transcribed from Tape Recording, Toronto, Ontario, Canada.

H. Richard T. Miller*, 1979, 'Star Wards,' The Solar Cross Foundation, CA.

I. John Reeves*, 03-1965, 'Interplanetary Language,' Brookville, FL.

J. Tuella, 1984, 'The Universal Concerto,' Guardian Action Publications, Durango, CO.

K. Partana Vegan*, 1963, 'Saturn Speaks,' reprinted by Health Research, Inc.

L. George Hunt Williamson, 1953, 'Other Tongues - Other Flesh,' Amherst Press.

M. George Hunt Williamson, 1954, 'The Saucers Speak,' New Age Publishing Co.

INNER LIGHT PUBLICATIONS PRESENTS
A TRIBUTE TO TUELLA

PRIMARY CHANNEL FOR THE ASHTAR COMMAND

Though she has passed from the physical realm, the channel Tuella remains the primary source of messages transmitted from the *Ashtar Command* , a spiritually advanced group of ETS who guide and instruct from a huge mother-ship circulation the earth at the equator. Before her transition to heavenly realms Inner Light purchased the rights to her monumental works and have endeavored to make them available to the public. The following titles are available directly from the publisher.

◑ *Ashtar: Revealing the Secret Identity of the Forces of Light and Their Spiritual Program For Earth*

Here are messages from Ashtar. spokesperson for the Solar Council whose mission is to assist in our growth as planetary individuals and to offer warnings and advice in these monumental times. A delightful read for advancing souls! - $15.00

◑ *Project World Evacuation   (9th Printing)*

Will we be lifted off the planet in times of global disaster by friendly space beings lead by members of the Ashtar Command. Is this the rapture spoke of in the Bible? Where will the rescued be taken. What are we expected to bring with us during the exodus? - $21.95

◑ *A New Book Of Revelations*

Exposes the true meaning of 666. The special significance of the 13th Vortex. Corrects many inaccurate translations made of the Old and New Testaments and lays the foundation for a New World. - $16.00

⟡ Cosmic Telepathy: A How To Manual

A workbook and study guide to expand your inner clairvoyant powers. Now it is possible for humans to transport the barriers of time and space. Special material added by T. Lobsang Rampa. Large format. 8x11 edition. $25.00

⟡ Cosmic Prophecies For The Year 2000

World chaos. World Changes. Freak Weather. Space Guardians. A cosmic symposium of 27 ET communiqués including 9 noted space commanders and representatives of the solar tribunal and spiritual hierarchy. $14.00

⟡ On Earth Assignment (Available Once Again!)

The cosmic awakening of light workers, Walk-Ins, Star Children has begun! Are you a reincarnated soul? Were you on Atlantis? Find out what your miss on earth is. $21.95

⟡ The Space People Speak

While not a Tuella book, this Ashtar Command presentation is one of the original offerings of west coast channels and contains spiritually received portraits of some of the Ashtar representatives created by Carol Ann Rodriguez. $12.00

Rare Collectors Item Now Available!

⟡ The Mystic Symbol Of The Solar Cross

Believed "lost" this rare manuscript has been impossible to obtain. Limited reprint for serious students ONLY. Here are the key symbols that offer us the basic laws government every phase of our awareness. Here is the Great Awakening that will enable us to evolve toward a consciousness of the basic oneness of all life. Over 250, 8x11 pages in perfect bound format. Book comes with CD of a lecture given by Tuella. Many have been looking for this book!

$39.95 (counts as two books for purposes of shipping)

Add $5 for shipping and handling for up to 3 titles.
All items in this ad just
$139.95 + $10.00 shipping and handling.
Place your order with:
Inner Light, Box 753, New Brunswick, NJ 08903
Credit Card Orders: 732-602-3407
PayPal Email: MrUFOS@hotmail.com

The idea behind Bible Magick is simple; all verses in the Bible are charged with spiritual energies. This power of creation is called "LOGOS," meaning "WORD." It is thought that God the Creator used the LOGOS to initiate creation.

The Universe and everything within it are divine words that have solidified. You can imagine that they were once dissolved in the sound vibrations of the divine cosmic word. Each thing we see is a divine word become solid.----------------------------**$18.00**

THERE IS A SECRET TO PERFORMING MAGICK!

THIS UNIQUE, VERY PERSONAL, BOOK OF SHADOWS, WILL TEACH YOU THIS CLOSELY GUARDED SECRET, SO THAT YOU CAN BECOME SUPER ENPOWERED WHEN PERFORMING ANY SPELL OR RITUAL.

$21.95

Made in the USA
Middletown, DE
07 October 2022

12226612R00144